How to Get Out of Your Own Way

HOW TO
GET OUT OF YOUR
OWN WAY

Inspiration and Transformational Techniques
to Open Space for Miracles

KRISTINA SISU

Book Cover Design: Marla Thompson
Typeset: Greg Salisbury

DISCLAIMER: This book discusses various healing methods and spiritual techniques utilized by the author, her family, colleagues and friends. It does not recommend any medical or spiritual course of action for your specific needs. For any medical concerns, and prior to following any alternate methods of healing, please first consult your medical and spiritual practitioners of choice.
Readers of this publication agree that neither Kristina Sisu nor her publisher will be held responsible or liable for damages that may be alleged or resulting directly or indirectly from their use of this publication.

To Annie, my soul sister. Thanks for your constant loving support;

to Denise and Carrie, who are earth angels with the most expansive hearts that I have ever met;

to Lori, my camping buddy, whose quiet reassurance is always there for support;

to my fabulous travel companions, Holly and Sharon;

to my amazing grandchildren, Cole, Callie, Ethan, Brianna, and Lily, who always bring out the love in me!

And to the two new additions to my life; Bahati and Eliza

Thank you for making my life so rich. I feel truly blessed.

Acknowledgments

Writing a book can be all-consuming and it doesn't happen without lots of support. First off, I want to thank my family for their encouragement and practical support, especially my daughter in-law Vanessa Foster for her editing expertise and her inspirational ideas regarding the cover; my son Justin Foster for his technical skills with all the pictures; and my oldest son James Pierotti for the graphics in the Transformer section. What a talented family I have!

All my friends have been so supportive and helpful. I especially want to thank Holly Levac for all her guidance and help with reviewing my material and writing the Foreword, and for being there for me, every step of the way. I couldn't have done it without you, Holly!

To Gord Mains and Dave Shotrill for offering me quiet, safe havens to write. To Sherri Jackson for her initial edit and getting the manuscript presentable. You are all such lights in my life. I am truly grateful to be sharing this journey with you.

I have been blessed to belong to a spiritual community called the "Centre for Inspired Living". This support has helped me "stay the course", and David Jones, our minister, has been a wonderful teacher and such an open-hearted presence in my life.

A thank you to the many authors whose work has inspired me and especially Michael J. Lincoln, Ph.D (formerly known as Narayan Singh) for "Messages from the Body." This material has been significant for me and many of my clients in understanding the emotional underlay around physical symptoms and illness.

Of course, I thank all my clients over the years who have helped me grow and offered such wonderful material for this book. Thank You! Thanks also to everyone at Influence Publishing for their creative support and especially to Julie Salisbury for her inspiration and great ideas on how to get this book birthed.

Thank you all. I am so grateful for all the assistance and guidance.

Contents

Acknowledgments
Contents
Foreword
Preface
Introduction
How to Use this Book

Chapter 1: The End of the World As I Know It, and I Feel Fine 1
Chapter 2: Illusion or Reality 19
Chapter 3: The Mind: Ally or Foe 37
Chapter 4: Make Your Energy Work for You 53
Chapter 5: Go Inside 67
Chapter 6: Open the Pathway 73
Chapter 7: Being at One 85
Chapter 8: Creating What You Really Desire 93
Chapter 9: Lightening Up 107
Chapter 10: Getting Out of the Way 111
Chapter 11: Transformers to Create Space for Miracles 117
    Transformer 1—Breathing 120
    Transformer 2—Meditation 122
    Transformer 3—Scripting a New Story 124
    Transformer 4—Emotional Stress Release 126
    Transformer 5—Emotional Freedom Technique 128
    Transformer 6—Time to Make Room for Fun 132
    Transformer 7—Make a Love List 134
    Transformer 8—Ho'oponopono 136
    Transformer 9—Positive Position 138
    Transformer 10—Materialize and Dematerialize 140
    Transformer 11—Three Heart Energy Exercises 142
    Transformer 12—Vitality Point 144
    Transformer 13—Meridian Wash 146
    Transformer 14—Gratitude Journal 148
    Transformer 15—Tapas Acupressure Technique 150
    Transformer 16—Spirit Action 152
    Transformer 17—Practise Being Happy 154
    Transformer 18—Daily Abundance Log 156
    Transformer 19—Bliss Method 158
    Transformer 20—Magnet Exercise 160
    Transformer 21—Reach to the Heavens Stretch 162
    Transformer 22—Calf Pump 164

Transformer 23—Shoulder Points and Neck Points 166
Transformer 24—Stepping out of Chaos 168
Transformer 25—Face Massage... 170
Transformer 26—Balancing Buttons 172
Transformer 27—Create a Happy Thought for the Day 174
Transformer 28—Three Thumps 176
Transformer 29—PACE.. 178
Transformer 30—Changing Belief Patterns 180
Transformer 31—Creating Personal Space 182
Transformer 32—Music 184
Transformer 33—Celebrate 186
Transformer 34—Calling in the Angels.. 188
Transformer 35—Get Your Creative Juices Going.................................... 190
Transformer 36—Opening the Doors to Your God Self 192
Transformer 37—Giving 194
Transformer 38—Positive Points... 196
Transformer 39—Group Activities 198
Transformer 40—Seeking External Help.. 200

Closing... 203
Afterword... 205
Resources 209
Author Biography 211

Foreword

If you do not read any further, I want you to know that this book has put theory and practice together in a meaningful way for those of you who are SEARCHING.

We are all spirits having a human experience. Yes, we have a human body with bones and muscles and organs. We have a brain with all its intricacies and biochemistry. We have different personalities, an ego, different skin colours, an astrological sign, and our unique way of operating in the world. Yet with all our similarities and differences, when you really drill down to the core of each human being, we are all connected by spirit. Regardless of your beliefs or religious affiliation, there is way more to us than you think. And we are truly all brothers and sisters.

I have been a practicing registered nurse for over thirty-four years. I used to think all the answers to illness and healing were found within scientific and medical research. And yes, we have made great advances that have been miraculous. However, new research is emerging that speaks to our energy fields as a source of illness and a method of healing. Research is explaining what this field is about. Our energy field can even be mapped within and around the human body. This field can actually be measured in the same way that your heart rhythm can be measured by an electrocardiogram.

Probably, like many of you, I have had some wonderful, happy times in my life and some, well, hell on earth times. I went searching for answers to: Why is this happening to me? How can I get out of this? What do I do to make myself feel better? There are some things in life that traditional Western medicine does not seem equipped to handle. Hey, I can say that, because I worked in that system for many years.

So I went searching. If you have picked up this book, then you are searching too. I went through a serious depression, and medications and counsellors did the best they could do, but my progress was slow and painful. My breakthrough came by immersing myself in reading about any topic related to spirituality, energy healing, meditation, and the list goes on.

Then I met Kristina Sisu. Now that was not by coincidence. Nothing in life is a coincidence, even you picking up this book. Kristina has been a dear and trusted friend for years and has supported me in my life's challenges and completed therapeutic energy interventions on me that have had lasting effects. Her energy healing is unique and effective. I have learned so much from her and we have continued our life's journey together. Her compassion for human struggle and actions to help those in need have been profound.

In all my readings and research over the years, I have not found a book like the one you have in your hands. It offers you an insight into the operations of the energy field, the belief systems you hold, and the greater universe. Then, on top of that, you get to actually do something about it. You get a potpourri of self-interventions to improve your level of health and well-being. No, you do not have to sit in a physician's office for two hours or try to book an appointment that might take a week. You can do it today in an informative and fun way. The transformers (activities) offered here are easy and useful, and you can do them anywhere—well maybe not at a board meeting.

My life has dramatically changed with the knowledge presented in this book, by knowing Kristina and the practices you will be exposed to.

Peace, Love, and Harmony
Holly Levac RN, BScN

Preface

Growing up in Canada, I always felt on the "outside of things", as though I didn't really belong here. My heritage is of Finnish descent and I didn't speak English until I went to school at the age of five. My parents had just immigrated before I was born. I looked different, with funny bows in my hair, European clothes, and a beret my Mom made me wear. The other kids seemed so cool in their scarves and stylish clothes; head scarves were the style back then.

Life presented lots of challenges. My Mom was chronically depressed and the rage she expressed, at the unfairness of the cards she had been dealt, was mainly directed at me. I was the only other female in the house; therefore, I was a mirror image for her projections.

I grew up desperately trying to fix things and make them better, to no avail. I never felt I "measured up". I think this was the underlying draw that eventually led me to Social Work. I thought that maybe through this profession I could somehow "fix" myself.

Even with all the chaos and dysfunction in my life, I felt the seeds for actualization had been planted long ago, and I always had this sense that there was a connection between our physical and psychological states—that the body, heart, and mind are interconnected, and that when we are sick, there is a reason; it isn't just random or genetic. This notion was dismissed by others as nonsense. However, I had a knowing that this was the truth.

So when I was diagnosed with a chronic illness myself, I knew deep inside that there was more to the illness than what appeared on the surface. This was a huge turning point for me and motivated me to really look inside. It wasn't a pretty sight. However, the illness was the gift that pointed me in the right direction. With my knowing that my psychological state was contributing to the "dis-ease" of my body, I started my path inward. What a journey it has been. Using the three Cs—Courage, Commitment, and Consistency—I talk about in the book, I was able to free myself from this illness and go on to create my authentic self.

All the training I undertook, such as the nutrition, energy work, and self-realization courses, were initially to help me heal myself, but it became a career path that I became totally dedicated to. My passion became helping others see that there is more going on than their minds could conjure up, and supporting them to realize that they are capable of so much more. I did this through private sessions, corporate wellness-workshop facilitation, and teaching at a college. It was so gratifying to see others have "light bulb" moments, as I shared my story of how I got to a place of health.

Life, as it does, continued to offer up challenges such as divorce, financial instability, and the death of my parents, but I used it all to release the old story of who I thought I was and create a new version of myself. There were many "dark nights of the soul". but I always knew it was part of the journey to really discover who I am. During this period, I birthed my first book, Food and the Emotional Connection (Seraphine Publishing, © 2002). Writing was something that I never imagined I would do, since English is my second language. However, I felt compelled to share my story so others could see how they too could move past any obstacle.

In my role as a practitioner helping others and also witnessing my own journey, I could see the truth that we are often a cause of our own suffering. It is not the world that keeps "socking it to us", but rather it is we who hold ourselves back through low self-esteem and the negative beliefs and patterns that we carry around as our truths. Most of what we carry is just lies: what others have told us about ourselves.

I began to realize that I was capable of following all my dreams, no matter how alien they looked to others. In 2006 I responded to an intuitive nudge, gave up my healing facilitation business, and decided I wanted to follow a dream I had had when I was a teenager: to move out West and push a rolly bag around an airport. Aged fifty-six, I applied to WestJet Airlines and became a flight attendant! I sold everything, drove my sports car across Canada, and embarked on a totally new phase of my life. I even amazed myself in realizing that anything is possible when you just follow your inner knowing and take leaps of faith. When we connect to that divine life force that lies inside each of us, we can accomplish anything.

Life has been quite a ride since that leap of faith and has taken me back full-circle once again to doing the healing work I love. I had a knowing that this story of self-empowerment needed to be shared. I balked a bit at writing another book, but my inner voice was very loud and clear. I also felt that most books on the shelves give lots of theory, whereas I wanted to provide a tool box, practical applications for people to shift things on their own. These tools have played such a valuable role in taking me to an amazing place of contentment and abundance. So another book is now birthed!

My desire is that these tools and this story will help you discover how magnificent you are. Sometimes we just need a helping hand to shift our perceptions and create an open space for new awareness. I know we are all limitless when we just get out of our own way and let the life force of divine intelligence guide our journey.

Introduction

I asked myself: Why write another spiritual, self-help book about personal evolution when bookstore shelves are overflowing with them? And the Universe whispered back: because people usually know what they should do, but often get stuck in how to do it. People get overwhelmed at how to turn an idea into reality, and then, it floats away on a cloud of frustration and self-doubt.

This is not a new concept. Science is echoing the ancient truth that the human mind is the ultimate prison. Programmed in the mind's information field are behaviours that bind us like manacles and chains. These behaviours come from our genetic makeup, our life experiences, the way we are parented, and the messages we have received about the world and ourselves. This is what gets in our way! We are too often tied up in knots, a matrix of negative beliefs that we are incapable of achieving our dreams or fulfilling our destiny.

Here's the truth: The only person who keeps your dreams from coming true is you! You are the one who holds yourself back and makes excuses to keep yourself within your own comfort zone. We often choose to blame others, or our parents, or our circumstances, instead of allowing ourselves the freedom to believe we can do, be, or have anything we desire. We get in our own way! It sounds silly, but everybody does it!

When I started planning this book, I asked my dear friends what they would need in a self-help book, if it was to be any use to them. What they shared was that they intellectually had the big picture and all the theories, but what they needed was an "instruction manual" that would simplify the journey. Something that would offer tools to support them when they hit a bump in the road, as we all do at some point. They were looking for strategies to help them get out of their own way, and reminders to be kind to themselves. They wanted to be reassured that where they are is exactly where they're meant to be at this time. They wanted tools to help them recognize and soar over any hurdles that sprung up on them in moments of fear, anger, or anxiety. They wanted techniques to rid themselves of negative patterns and emotions that were blocking their success, sometimes in ways they were not even consciously aware of. I have written this book with all of these things in mind; therefore this book is unique in that it offers you specific strategies and not just theory. In these pages you will find ways to actually release this old baggage and get out of your own way to allow the divine force that is the truth of who you really are to shine. You will learn how simple acupressure points can transform your old ways of thinking in minutes or how to tap certain acupressure points that can give you more energy and vitality and help you refocus. Bet you never thought something as simple as tapping, or stretching, could change your life forever. This and much more is what you will discover in this book.

After going from desperation and struggle to living a life of more ease and contentment, I believe that I have something to contribute to the world that will help people feel better, and live happier, more fulfilled lives. My intention in life has always been to empower people to create and follow their own amazing paths, and to offer tools to change the unhealthy patterns that keep us stuck; patterns that limit our innate ability to soar and be all we can be. We are so busy doing, controlling, scheming, and planning that we create the very obstacles that we are trying to avoid. Then we wonder why we're so unhappy and unfulfilled.

This book is full of inspiring stories that I hope will touch your heart and show you that anything is possible. The chains and manacles that bind us can be released and we can escape our own self-made prisons. Healing illness, creating financial stability, and realizing our dreams are within each of our grasps. We just need to get out of our own way and trust the inner power that we all have to draw to us that which enhances and makes our life richer.

In this book, I will introduce you to a concept called "Transformers". These Transformers are practical ideas, activities, and exercises, that anyone can do; they will actually change the energy patterns that are holding you back. Simply put, these Transformers will help you get out of your own way. After all, the only thing that's stopping you from being, having, and doing everything you ever wanted in life is YOU!

This book will provide you with inspirational stories, guidance, Transformers (practical techniques), and reassurance to help to make your journey easier. You are capable of amazing things. Every choice we make either builds a stepping stone or a stumbling block in our life. We all have the power to make our life heaven or hell. I choose heaven and if this is also your choice, then I hope that this book is a road map to help get you there.

"The greatest revolution in our generation is that of human beings, who by changing the inner attitudes of their minds, can change the outer aspects of their lives," Marilyn Ferguson.

How to Use this Book

This book is filled with stories, guidance, and ideas to help you realize what you are truly capable of. To help you on this journey, the Transformers in Chapter 11 are specific tools and techniques that can change an energy pattern and help you move forward. Transformers are available on separate pages, so that if you are perplexed as to which one to use, you can use your innate wisdom to go to the page that is right for you. This is like "therapy in a book" and you can trust your inner intuition to lead you to the page you need most at that moment. Some of the Transformers are actual acupressure techniques that have a profound effect by releasing and shifting energy, and others are tools to help you redirect your focus and help you create a new way of being in the world that can make your journey much easier. This will be like having your own built in therapist for guidance and support.

Keeping a journal will be helpful as you read this book. You can make notes and answer some of the questions, or just keep track of some of the exercises and how they affected you. Writing is a powerful tool to get stuff out of your head and release it. If you are setting intentions, then writing them down can be like making a contract with yourself, sealing them in ink.

You may also want to read this book with a partner or friend so you can practise some of the Transformers together and share the journey. Sharing this experience with someone who is also interested in moving forward in their lives can be very powerful. Playing with some of these tools can be great fun. So stay open to your own observations, thoughts, and reactions. There is no wrong way—just have fun and then observe the changes. They can be subtle or dramatic. How energy shifts will be unique for each person.

Growing and learning doesn't need to be arduous. Open to your inner wisdom and create a new way of seeing yourself. Start telling yourself a new story about your life. Get bored with the same old messages your mind plays over and over. See yourself as powerful and joyful. When your mind natters at you, just set your attention on the creative, Divine force whispering in the background; it resides in all of us. Focus on the miracles that are waiting for you if you'd just get out of your own way!

Chapter 1

The End of the World As I Know It, and I Feel Fine

The World Is as We See It or Is It?

Sitting across from the doctor as he announced my fate, I was stunned. "You have a chronic disease for which there's no cure," he said.

I had been in incredible pain for almost a year and a half; there were no answers as to why. No one could answer that one simple question: why? I was devastated. What seemed at the time to be an end to my life as I had known it was actually a beginning, an incredible gift for which I would be forever grateful. It would be the catalyst that forced me into unraveling the mess that I had gotten myself into. In the end, it would bring me closer to who I really am and take me on adventures I had never dreamed of.

Let's go back a bit to how I had got myself to that point.

I was a very frazzled social worker, often working twelve-hour days and sitting on many community committees. I had a young family, a large house with a large mortgage to match, and a stress load that was destroying my body. My body was talking, but nobody was listening until it got tired of talking and started acting out its dis-ease. My doctor diagnosed Interstitial Cystitis, an autoimmune disorder that attacks the lining of the bladder. Now, immune disorders are interesting. They are essentially the body attacking itself, treating itself as a foreign substance; an invader! Wow, that says a lot about how connected I was to my own body, my needs, and my thoughts. I was racing through my life, doing everything I thought I was supposed to for everybody else, and ignoring the red flags my body was throwing at me to say, "Stop!"

Well, my body finally had had enough and said, "If you're not going to choose to stop, I'll make you stop." And, I suddenly woke up.

1

I had to take a very long, hard look at how I had gotten to this place. Luckily I am stubborn and rarely accept someone else's truth as my own. I refused to take this diagnosis as my fate. I chose to see my world differently. The doctor told me that surgery was my best option, but I decided quickly that I was not having a surgery that would leave me wearing a urostomy bag for the rest of my life. I set the intention that I was going to start paying acute attention to my body, and I was going to heal myself from this dis-ease. The first steps were learning how to breathe deeply and meditate. Transformers 1 and 2 (see Chapter 11) are now an integral part of my daily life.

Friends who thought they were being kind said I wasn't being realistic, but I am grateful that I didn't listen to their fearful advice. I stayed true to my intention and the inner voice that knew there was another way. Now, twenty years later without surgery, I am healthy, vibrant and in awe of this life I have created. This is my story and it may not work for others. We each have our own journey.

The Healing Process

Healing illness and pain can be a spiritual journey as mine was. It can be the "calling card" that calls you home to who you really are. There is such fluidity to this journey when we allow ourselves to follow the flow, to go easily with what comes up next and not force this journey we call life. Let the hand of your higher wisdom guide you gently to your pain and guide you again to walk through it. Honour it, but do not let it define who you are, because you are so much more, so much more than you could possibly imagine. Any pain or illness can be a gift that can set you free.

From my experience it took the three Cs to heal my illness: courage, commitment, and consistency.

Courage

Courage refers to the courage to go inside and see the demons that could lead to a "dark night of the soul"; the courage to go beyond our comfort zone and see who we really are.

Commitment

Commitment refers to running the course and staying true to yourself. You have to hold the intention close to your heart and not waver from it. You have to commit to doing whatever it takes to help you heal, and make the commitment that if you slip you are willing to get "back on the horse" and stay true to your intention no matter what it takes. Remember to be gentle with yourself as you find your own way.

Not everyone can find this commitment.

The doctor I had seen witnessed my healing and gave me the names of five people who had the same disease so that I could share with them what I had learned, mainly about the nutrition component. The "diet" was very strict and out of all the five people, not one was willing to make the commitment, especially when they found out they could no longer drink Pepsi!

Consistency

Consistency means you can't just eat right for a few days and then let it all go and return back to your old patterns. You have to be consistent with whatever healing regime you choose and consistent in going inside to make the changes that are required. It took me two years to totally heal that illness.

Now, I do think healing can happen instantaneously, but that wasn't my journey. The journey is as unique as we each are and only you know what is right for you.

I have a close friend with whom I have a real sister bond. It's actually quite mystical. Her first name is Anne and her second name is Lillian. My sister who died before I was born was named Anneli—the same first name combined with the first two letters of my friend's second name. We are repeatedly asked if we are sisters.

What is even more synchronistic is that one day Anne called and wanted to know the symptoms to my disease. At this point, we were living in different areas of Canada, and hadn't seen each other for a while. My symptoms were identical to what she was experiencing. What are the odds? It is not that common an ailment.

I was very grateful that I was able to share with Anne what I had done to heal and we stayed in close contact while she also healed from this illness. Her journey was also an inner one: though her emotional responses were a bit different from mine, the gist of the journey was the same. She stayed true to the three Cs, and is now healthy, happy, and well.

So now there are two of us (and I hope many more) who have moved past this "incurable disease" called Interstitial Cystitis.

For some people, recovering from an illness isn't their journey. Though we all want recovery for those we love, their story may be quite different. For some, the healing still happens, but not on a physical level. An amazing client I knew died of AIDs, but she was healed, not in the physical sense, but spiritually; she was at peace and went gracefully. For others, it is their journey to let their illness be the vehicle that takes them to the other side. Each person's story is unique and needs to be honoured without judgment. Just send love on whatever path they choose.

Setbacks Can Result From "Stinking Thinking"

What appears in front of us as a setback is not always what it seems. It may just be a door to take you to another place where you never realized you could go. It is the courage to open the door and go through that can make all the difference. The trick is to believe in yourself and learn to tame the constant ramble that can be our "stinking thinking", and see past our limiting patterns and beliefs. This is where I would like to take you; to a place where miracles are a common occurrence and where you get so far out of your own way you may not even recognize yourself.

Where Did this Stinking Thinking Come From?

I believe we are all part of a collective consciousness of ancestral origin, a kind of psychic DNA, full of patterns and beliefs that make our blueprint and can have the overwhelming potential to squash our dreams and keep us thinking small. Added to this collective are our own individual patterns and conditioning, which come from family, genetics, culture, and society at large, and that create the belief system by which we live, a sort of biosphere where we believe things must be a certain way in order for us to survive.

Author and lecturer Gregg Braden writes on page 233 of *Spontaneous Healing of Belief*, "There are numerous case histories that suggest that the power of a belief can be inherited if it's accepted and held by others. The studies show that beliefs can even be passed on from one generation to the next. If they're positive and life affirming, the ability to perpetuate them for many generations is a good thing. If, on the other hand they are limiting and life denying, they can cut short the experience that we cherish so deeply yet often take for granted: that of life itself."

On page 26, he says, "our most influential programs have mainly been acquired from others and do not necessarily support our own personal goals and aspirations. In fact, many of our strengths and weaknesses, the parts of ourselves we own as who we are, are directly attributed to familial and cultural perceptions downloaded into our minds before we were six years old." Perceptions acquired before age six become the fundamental subconscious programs that shape the character of an individual's life. While we are doing all this downloading we are not at the stage where we are involved in critical thinking. We are just sponges absorbing all that is around us. If what is around us is positive and healthy, that's good. But when it's not, it does tremendous damage. When, as children, we downloaded limiting and sabotaging beliefs, those perceptions and misperceptions become our truth.

"If our platform is one of misperception our subconscious mind dutifully generates behaviours that are coherent with those programmed truths. Perceptions acquired during this pivotal developmental period can actual override genetically endowed instincts" (ibid page 39). For instance, we all have instincts to swim. Why then are so many people afraid of water? It is a learned behaviour during this crucial time in our lives.

And we believe these perceptions are our truth.

Even more profound is the influence our negative thinking, belief, and perceptions have not only on our behaviour, but on our very gene activity. Perceptions not only control our behaviour, they control gene activity as well. This revised version of science emphasizes the reality that we actively control our genetic expression moment to moment. Therefore rather than perceiving ourselves as helpless victims to our genes, we must now accept and own the empowering truth that our perceptions and responses to life dynamically shape our biology and behaviour.

It is a powerful, life-changing truth that we have a lot more control over our destiny then we ever thought possible. The good news is that whatever has been programmed can be deprogrammed and all it takes is one person, in any generation, to heal the limiting beliefs. In doing so, we not only change ourselves but obliterate that limiting belief for generations to come.

So it seems that we as individuals have very little to do with forming the way we see our world, until we become conscious and begin to ask questions like, "Whose rules are those anyway?", "Whose stinking thinking is that?", "Whose voice is that in my head?", "Who is actually driving my bus?", and most importantly, "Whose beliefs am I actually living by?"

In my own personal life, I felt like my childhood was about collecting all this limiting thinking that had been passed (or dumped) on to me, and then spending the rest my life working at releasing it in order to fully understand who I really am. When I started doing my personal healing, I began to learn, or rather, remember, that I was a limitless source of creation and the more I got out of my own way the more I seemed to be in tune with this fundamental truth. Miracles happened for me, and things that I never thought I could do I was doing with ease and grace. It's old, primordial thinking that gets in the way of our greatness. The voices saying, "You are not good enough, you can't do it, you don't belong," and, we have heard them for so long, they feel like undeniable facts to our brainwashed minds.

Our limiting, negative thinking can also mean life or death. I had two friends who were diagnosed with terminal cancer. The doctor told one friend that he had three months to live and yes, in three months he was gone. The other friend, who was given a similar diagnosis but no exact time line, chose to think differently about her circumstance. She lived for one and a half years. I thought it was so amazing that what you believe about your illness and what someone tells you can affect how long you live, or even whether you live or die.

The lies we tell ourselves can rule our lives until we examine exactly what is going on in our brains and take charge of changing them.

Let me explain how these patterns become entrenched. In the emotional part of our brain is the *amygdala*, which acts like a tiny computer chip, storing all memories from this life, and perhaps beyond this life to other lives we may have lived and memories from those lives that are pertinent to our lessons in this one. One of the functions of the amygdala is to organize what becomes familiar and relate it to previous memories and experiences that it has stored. If a person lives in an environment that is chaotic, unpredictable, or highly stressful, the rhythm patterns generated by the heart become discordant and incoherent. "The amygdala learns to treat disharmony as familiar; thus the child, especially the young child, feels at home with incoherence (chaos), which really is discomfort. It feels normal to the child. On the basis of what has become familiar to the amygdala, the frontal cortex mediates decisions as to what is appropriate or not in any given situation. Thus, subconscious emotional memories underlie and affect our perceptions, emotional reactions, and thought processes," (*Science of The Heart*, www.heartmath.org).

If you have experienced chaos early in life, it will feel like the norm and you will make choices that support this old pattern. In other words, you'll choose behaviours that create chaotic outcomes, even if you consciously believe you are choosing the opposite. Your body physically predicts and expects chaos as a normal state of being.

Check in with your life experiences and reflect on your own life to see if that rings true for you.

The good news is that these patterns can be reprogrammed so that coherence (calm) becomes the normal and comfortable state.

Stinking Thinking

The more your physical body is in a happy state the easier it is to handle the "stinking thinking" and the stress that comes from that. I notice that when I have not been able to exercise, meditate, sleep well and eat well it totally affects how I deal with my ego. This is when I tend to revert back to my "default mode". A default mode is an old pattern that your ego is comfortable with and will easily fall back into when you are unconscious, or stressed. For me, my default mode is "doing" based on my ego's need to control. It's also when I am more likely to revert to worrying, which is another default mode for me. As soon as I get back on track, it is so much easier to stay peaceful and to control the limiting thinking.

Take a moment to think about what your default mode is. Where does your mind tend to go when you are tired and not feeling balanced? Is it a place of worry? Maybe eating or an addiction could be your default mode. When you revert to default, cut yourself some slack; be kind and gentle with yourself, but set a clear intention to get back on track. Know where your weak spots are and you are more likely to recognize them before they take over, making it easier to get back into a balanced state again.

The next technique I focused on to heal myself from my dis-ease was improving my thinking. See Transformer 3—Scripting a New Story.

Taking Charge of our Stinking Thinking

I am not sure that we can completely eradicate our BS—our bullshit—the lies we tell ourselves, but we can take our power away from its grip on us. Our BS is simply the stories we have told ourselves that create the stinking thinking; we can change the stories.

We create our own obstacles by all the stories we tell ourselves that aren't true. Like the old line, "creating mountains out of mole hills". We need to create new stories and write a new script that is empowering. (See a neat example in the Transformers section, Transformer 3—Scripting a New Story.)

Gregg Braden says this beautifully: "What could be more empowering than the ability to change the world and our lives simply by altering what we believe in our hearts and minds? Such a power sounds like stuff of fairy tales. Maybe that's precisely why we are so drawn to such fantasies. They awaken the memory that sleeps inside us of our power in the world and our ability to create our own reality." (ibid, page 91).

When we take charge by acknowledging our negative emotions that come from limiting thinking, we can make different choices and not allow such thinking to take our power away from us. Author and neuro-anatomist Jill Bolte Taylor says this very well: "I'm running my anger circuit. I don't like the way it feels in my body, because it's destructive to my health and my stress level. So I'm going to pass it away. I'm going to let it do its thing for 90 seconds and then move on. Owning your power owns your triggers." (*Spirituality and Health*, May-June, 2009, page 75).

When we are in our limiting thinking it is like we are bleeding our energy away. When we release it and are in our Divine essence, we shift to a place of receiving. So we can either be bleeding or receiving: the choice is always ours.

I admit sometimes our triggers can have a tenacious hold on us and that is why I have given you Transformers in Chapter 11, like Transformer 4—Emotional Stress Release and Transformer 5—Emotional Freedom Technique, so you have tools to use to change the energy.

Stinking thinking involves triggers and stories that we tell ourselves and in most cases they aren't even true. That's why I like to call it BS, the lies that we tell ourselves that we got from others. We all have this running diatribe in our heads. Here are some examples:

"I have a hard time losing weight."

"I never get the job."

"I'm getting older so I guess my sight will start to fail." (There are tons of stories around aging).

"It always rains when I go camping."

"I'm no good at (or I can't do) _____."

"There is no gain without pain." (Boy, who created this one! I personally think suffering is overrated.)

Can you relate to any of these?

These one-liners can create stories that become self-fulfilling prophecies. We are so full of self-fulfilling prophecies for ourselves and prophecies for others that we don't leave room for change. We have already determined how it is going to be. I see this a lot with parents and their children: "He won't eat that". Well, if you keep saying that then you're right, he won't eat that. It's bad enough that we have all this daunting old junk in our subconscious, but we continually make up new junk. We need to speak with intent so we leave the doors open for change. We need to be careful of what we create with our words.

I was recently with a friend and we were talking about her weight. She said, "It doesn't seem to matter what I do. Nothing works."

"Wow," I thought, "how is 'nothing works' working for you? Obviously not well."

Once we explored it further, my friend could see that this story of "nothing works" had to change. It's helpful to see what is underneath a story, so we can get to the root of why we are telling ourselves falsehoods. In my friend's case, I eventually found out that it was all about the need to protect herself.

I told a story to myself once that turned into a very unpleasant situation. My story was "I cannot do a long drive by myself". So out of fear I got a man I knew to come with me on the long drive. Well, it was a disaster. He was full of fear himself and got stressed very easily. Then, in the middle of seven lanes of traffic in Miami, he threw the map in the air and said, "I can't do this." So there I was in the dark, manoeuvring through seven lanes to pull over and try to figure out where to go. Needless to say, I did the drive back by myself and it was a piece of cake. So I stopped telling myself that story and now long drives by myself are not an issue anymore.

The stories in your head are just that: stories. They are not the truth. They're not real. They actually have no power. Just like that monster in your closet when you were a kid. It's all a story you created. Change them and create new, positive stories. Start creating new stories and challenge every story you have ever told yourself about who you are and what you can accomplish. These new stories can be catalysts for liberating yourself and they will lead you to joy, not fear.

The more we clean up our mind, the more we connect to our Divine intelligence, our God Self, our "I am" presence, or whatever term you choose to use to describe this connection to the creative source of all that is. Our beliefs are at the core of how we live our lives.

"Good thoughts and actions can never produce bad results; bad thoughts and actions can never produce good results. This is but saying that nothing can come from corn but corn, nothing can come from nettles but nettles. Men understand this law in the natural world, and work with it; but few understand it in the mental world (though its operation there is just as simple and undeviating," writes philosophical writer James Allen in *As a Man Thinketh*.

Let me be clear here: some of your beliefs are also unconscious; they are part of that collective consciousness that you may not even be aware that you have. A clue is what is showing up in your life. For example, if money is scarce in your life and you are always struggling, then there is a belief somewhere in your mind that is keeping you from abundance. You may not even be aware of this thought consciously, but, you are drawing scarcity to you. So just look at what is showing up in your life and ask yourself, "What belief could I have that is drawing this circumstance to my life?"

Dr. Willard Fuller says this so clearly: "We walk in the atmosphere of our own believing." (as quoted in the book by Daniel W. Fry, Ph.D., *Can GOD Fill Teeth?*).

What we believe is what we create

Creating "happy thoughts" takes practice. You can't change a lifetime of negative thinking over night, but the more you practise being happy, the more you change your hardwiring to this new thought form and the easier life becomes. One way is to wake up in the morning and choose a happy thought for the day. (See Transformer 27—Create a Happy Thought for the Day.) When your mind starts with its litany of BS, consciously remember your happy thought. Make it a powerful one that has good feelings attached to it and practise, practise, practise.

One happy thought I use is about a time when I lived beside a lake and one day, it was pure ice. My neighbour had a four-wheel-drive truck, and he drove his wife and me out to the middle of the lake on our skates. We had a large Canadian flag to hold between us and the wind just blew us back to the shore. Oh, my goodness, it was fun! I felt such freedom in my heart as we did this over and over until our red cheeks and cold hands told us it was time to go in. That thought will quickly change any negative thought for me. I have created many of these happy thoughts that all have intensely good feelings attached. Thinking of times with my grandkids can also bring me right back to my heart and a happy thought.

So, take a good look at your life. What are some of your beliefs that are impacting you? The following are some examples. Just read them and see how each feels. Is there some truth there for you? If you are not sure, then consider the opposite. For example, for the thought "life is hard", the opposite is "life is easy". Is that true for you? Make a list to keep track of your beliefs. You can use the Transformers to start shifting these.

Here are some beliefs about the world and our place in it:

- Life is hard.
- Change is hard.
- There is not enough to go around.
- There is not enough love.
- There is not enough money.
- Life is random and material.
- Original sin exists (Humanity is guilty).
- Pessimism (it will never get better).
- The world is a mess.
- As we get older, our health deteriorates.
- Menopause is difficult.

Here are some beliefs about ourselves:

- I am not good enough.
- Speaking my truth is not safe.
- I can't help it.
- Anger is dangerous.
- Asking for help shows weakness.
- Feeling my feelings is scary.
- I am boring.
- I am lazy.
- I am not very intelligent.
- To be spiritual, I need to be poor.
- I am trapped by my past.
- I get sick easily.
- I'm dependent on others.
- I am unlovable.
- I am a fraud.
- I have no control over my weight.
- I am not attractive.
- I'm unhappy.
- I am weaker than they are.
- I don't deserve money; or love; or abundance; or success.

- I must keep a low profile.
- The body is inferior to the spirit.
- I must avoid difficulty, because this will relieve my pain.
- I am not worthy.
- I am a victim.
- Facing my pain will lead to my destruction.
- I will never get ahead.

Here are some beliefs about other people:

- People cannot be trusted.
- Men are superior.
- People are out to get you.
- People always leave.
- Women are not to be trusted.
- People are only out for what they can get.
- They are against me.
- They are wrong, I am right.
- I must protect myself from others because they will hurt me.
- I need a relationship to feel whole.

Now that you have reviewed the list, you'll have an idea of what kinds of thoughts are true for you, at least in your conscious mind. How are these affecting your life? Do you want to release them, or are they comfortable? The ego doesn't like change and sometimes if you have been living with a pattern for a long time, you may meet resistance in wanting to let it go. Just stay true to your intentions and don't give the negative patterns any fuel. Eventually they will wither and die. Like an unwanted house guest—if you don't feed them, they go elsewhere!

What Coloured Glasses Are You Seeing Life Through?

Our beliefs, collective consciousness, and experiences that we have accumulated along our path form our individual perceptions. Our beliefs are like the lenses in our glasses that we see the world through. With these perceptions, we form our judgments and interpretations of our life and also everyone else's. The ego loves to judge, not only others, but also ourselves. The ego loves to feel superior and in control. What is right, what is wrong, who is right, who is wrong? It is a constant we all engage in. Until we recognize judgments are major obstacles that get in the way of pure consciousness being able to flow to us, they can keep us stuck and closed off to the magic.

The Hero and the Thief

I have a dear friend who defines her free self and her ego by using the terms "The Hero" and "The Thief". I love this analogy, because it is so clear. When we are in the ego/personality, it is robbing us of our true potential and our joy. It truly is a thief. The thief is the part of us that buys into the lies and sees it as our truth. It will bring up your past failures in a flash to remind you of your limitations. It will give you lots of fear when you want to do something new or beyond your present expectations of yourself. It will remind you of all the "what ifs" that could go wrong. It's really good at that. It steals away your future.

Now the hero is your divine intelligence, highest self, or God Self, or whatever term you want to use. It is the part of us that is engaged with our heart and knows what is in our highest good. It was my hero that I drew on to heal my illness and my hero I called on to make all the many big leaps of faith that I have made to move forward and leave my past behind. It's my hero that healed my relationships and saw that I had amazing potential that I had only begun to tap into. When we are in the hero mode, we are aligned with creation and can see beyond the limitations of the ego/personality. The hero is limitless consciousness.

Nobody I know has engaged their hero self in their journey as much as a particular friend of mine. She was diagnosed with bone cancer and actually had it twice; both times she used her hero to heal her illness and to become an amazing inspiration to others. The second time, she had just come to Canada from Ireland. She had only been here for a short time when the cancer reared its ugly head again. This was a very difficult time and she was in excruciating pain, but again she drew on her hero and higher forces to support her. She was very clear with the Universe on how she saw her life unfolding: cancer in her bones was not part of that unfolding. She looked deeply at where she had limited herself, and used her intuitive senses guided by the divine force within to attract therapies and external supports to find the healing path that was right for her alone. Her journey has inspired me and many others, and has made me realize just what we are actually capable of. We truly are limitless beings!

We all have the power to engage our hero and overcome trials and tribulations in our lives. That to me is what is so exciting about this journey. How you do this will be individual to you and now you have the tools to do this with.

The Ego and Its Role

I do want to clear something up about the ego before we continue, because I know it sounds like I am ego/personality bashing. The real intention isn't to get rid of the ego, which you can't do anyway—it is part of us and has a valuable role and function. What we do need is for the ego to come into balance, where it isn't totally running the show, but more at the service of our higher, divine selves. I also think a helpful way to deal with the ego is not through anger or frustration at its antics, but with kindness and love. Like tough love with a teenager. You need to be firm but also kind and honour its role. Frustration just creates more fuel for the ego. So be kind and gentle with yourself as you transcend the ego and guide it to come into balance with the true nature of your being.

Letting Go of the Past and Vacuuming up Your Ancestors

A dramatic example of how letting go of the past can have such a profound effect came from a former student of mine in a college course I taught called "Don't worry: Be happy". This student really stood out. When he arrived he got himself settled, arms crossed over his chest and a not-so-happy look on his face. I thought, "I will definitely earn my salary with this class." Most of the people in the class were tired of feeling stressed all the time and wanted to feel happier and lighter. This gentleman seemed pretty set in his ways and I was not sure what kind of progress he would make. One night we discussed how past resentments can be holding us back and creating so much suffering in our lives, how letting go and forgiving is essential to moving forward. This particular lesson seemed to really pique this student's interest. He shared that he could see how he had been holding onto a very old resentment toward his wife and that it affected all parts of his life.

Using the information he gained in the course, he made a courageous choice to face this demon and to let it go. By the end of our seven-week course, he was a different man. He was laughing, and said even the folks at work had wondered what had happened to change him so dramatically. The whole class agreed that he was very different, and the huge smile on his face was evidence of this change. All he did was let old resentments go. They can have a powerful and tenacious hold and freeing them will set you free to live the life you are meant to live. This student was a wonderful example of how profound one simple choice can be.

In my personal experience I have seen that so much of the baggage that I have carried has also been carried by all my ancestors, and I was just lugging around the same junk they had. It felt at times like a heaviness so palpable, it was like a black cloud that was following me around. On one of my trips home to my country of origin, Finland, I could see how prevalent this was in the society. Depression and alcohol abuse were very common. My family all seemed to have a very stoic nature and kept their feelings locked tightly inside. I remember once when I was a teenager visiting my family that I was the only one screaming when we went on a roller coaster—everyone else was very stoic. I was the weird Canadian cousin.

If you take a look at the history of my homeland, Finland, you'll see struggle and strife form much of its history. It has lost forty-two wars! It is also dark from September to May with very little sunlight, and sunlight is where we get our Vitamin D from. The lack of sunlight and Vitamin D can have quite negative effects on the brain. This disorder is called S.A.D. (seasonal affective disorder); it can be very common among people who live wherever there is a lot of darkness and limited sunlight.

My family in particular had suffered much, with many family losses; poverty consciousness had been quite dominant.

I began to recognize how all this ancestral baggage was affecting every part of my life. I made a conscious choice and set an intention to let go of all these negative aspects that kept me in suffering and were not allowing me to reach my full potential. I set an intention that I was going to bring ease and joy into my life. I decided to "vacuum up" all these unhelpful cultural beliefs and reinvent myself. I can say without a doubt that the dark cloud is gone and the heaviness no longer resides in my heart. This was not an overnight process, but the result of years of holding what I desired for myself and continuously working on my energy system (using the Transformers in Chapter 11) to let the effects of my culture go.

What forms your background? What are you carrying around with you from your culture? Is your belief system aligned with your highest good, or is it skewed by what you've been led to believe?

Now I do want to explain that there can also be many positive aspects from our culture that we want to keep. In the Finnish language is the word *sisu*, which I adopted as my last name. It is pronounced "seesoo". A rough translation of *sisu* is "a determination to meet one's goals"; "a strength that is unwavering", sort of like *chutzpah*. I was divorced and no longer wished to keep my married name and my maiden name was complicated and hard to pronounce. I also knew that the new adventure of being single would take strength and fortitude. This name has served me very well. In my culture, there is an amazing fortitude that keeps the people from being suppressed and has allowed them to realize their independence as a country even with obstacles at every turn. This sisu fortitude has helped me through many difficult situations and is a trait I am glad I have adopted.

Chapter 2

Illusion or Reality

Who Are We Really?

Science and spirituality now seem to be saying the same thing: we are limitless; we can change the course of our lives by believing in ourselves and by focusing on what we truly desire. By this I don't mean all the rhetoric that we have heard about creating more stuff, which to me is just spiritual materialism. Stuff is great, but that is not what a truly rich and wondrous life is all about. Creating inner states that have life-enhancing qualities like peace, love, and expansion, and from these states all is possible. Stuff, if you choose stuff, is then just a by-product of all the wonderful healing states that you feel. Change the inner world and the outer world changes easily.

The life we live through our ego is really "a grand illusion" which, as my angelic friend Denise Hagan says in her song "For those who hear", "can be hard to live sometimes" (www.denisehagan.com). We can choose to hang on to the illusion or to see the grander reality that even science confirms.

In his book, *The Physics of Miracles*, chiropractor Dr. Richard Bartlett states: "At a fundamental level what we are all composed of is a stream of consciousness. All situations in life are merely patterns of light and information. If you want to change anything in your life, change the frequency, density, or quality of the light patterns that make up that reality."

What's fascinating to me is that we are the observers of our lives and have dramatic impact on how life manifests. "Some quantum physicist says that until a quantum system is consciously observed or measured, it remains in a superposition of multiple possibilities," (EnlightenNext Magazine). So we are not mere observers of our lives, but active participants in its unfolding.

As Gregg Braden puts so well in his book, *The Spontaneous Healing of Belief*: "We directly affect the waves and particles of the Universe. In short the Universe responds to our beliefs. When we observe we create and modify what is created. Sometimes the effect of our observation is nearly undetectable but sometimes it is not. Either way the discoveries of the last century suggest that our act of observing the world is an act of creation unto itself. And it's consciousness that's doing the creating." Put simply "The Universe is nonmaterial—it is mental and spiritual" (page 271).

Scientists seem to be saying that between the particles there is an empty space, which can be called "zero point energy" or "life force" or "God" or, as my friend David says, "the God particle". And we the observers—us—influence this empty God space. WOW!! Just imagine what you could accomplish if you held this truth close to your heart, got out of the way, and let your higher self be your guide. I like to think of this energy as the "eloquent master of intelligence". The more we can let our ego rest and let the magnificence of our essence direct our life, the easier and more amazing it becomes. Then you as your Divine God Self can become the master of your own experience. From this place, miracles are common place.

"The miracles of life are something that begins deep within us. They result from the truly astonishing ability to transform quantum energy into stuff of reality. The transformation happens through the power of our beliefs. (Transformation literally means beyond form). It all begins with our power to free ourselves from false limits of the past. Through the healing of our beliefs we discover how—with the grace and ease that comes from experiencing ourselves as part of the world rather than separate from it. We become the seed of life's miracles as well as the miracles themselves" (ibid page 163).

We are a powerful force in this world and most of us don't even know it. Once we realize and feel it in our hearts that the more we focus on the awe in our lives, then the more awe we will create. Life truly is magical but first we need to know what it is that gets in the way of this magic and find ways to release these blocks so we can live the life we truly desire and are meant to live. We are not meant to struggle. We were not created for this, and that's not what life's about. We have limitless potential; we just need to realize this.

An Insight

I had an insight from a meditation a while back, which really clarified what my real purpose is:

> My only purpose here is to surrender to my Divine essence, no goals, just surrender. And the reason it happens so slowly is it is so powerful we couldn't fathom it all at once. That's why growth happens bit by bit—it's all our human bodies can handle. Nothing else is required but to surrender and go with what comes up naturally and just be. Get off the roller coaster, which is the ego in action, and just watch and listen and follow any action you are inspired to do. The ego is just a way to express the Divine when you let the Divine be the guide.
>
> Living a life of surrender is like going where the wind blows you; saying "yes" to opportunities that present themselves; allowing yourself to experience the things that life offers you; not holding any preconceived notions about yourself, only hearing the whispers of your own truth.

This insight has been a guiding force for me and whenever the chatter of my "monkey mind" pops up and wants to plan and control, I remember my real purpose is just to get out of my own way and connect to the source and let it all unfold. This hasn't always been an easy process, but it's getting easier and easier when I remember who I really am: a part of creation, connected to the vital life force that created me. A powerful realization is that I am limitless.

The Mystical Side of Life

When I first started on this path of self-discovery and spiritual awareness, I was sick and very entrenched in my ego view that I was alone and had to heal my illness by myself. Religion had never been a huge part of my life as I was growing up and though our family went to church it was a very superficial kind of religious practice. When I married my then-partner, his family was evangelical with very strong views. From my perspective this religion seemed fear-based and judgmental; I stayed very far removed from it. The teachings of love and compassion that I understood as Christianity just didn't seem to be playing out in his family.

When I got ill, I felt very alone with no higher sense of myself to guide and help me heal. God, as I perceived it from a religious standpoint, didn't fit either. Finally I did realize that there was much more to my life than the physical body I was living in, and started drawing to me books and people to help me get clarity. One day, I was reading *Minding the Body, Mending the Mind*, by integrative-medicine pioneer Dr. Joan Borysenko. Through her poem, "Home to Your Inner Self," she explores how we reach our inner selves:

"They will give you safe passage, too
If you ask with faith,
even if it is the size of a mustard seed,
and if you are patient and willing to listen
to the directions of the Universe,
even if they are not what you want to hear.
Thy will, not mine be done—this is the understanding that will bring you Home".

I was so moved by these words and cried for myself when I realized I didn't need to do this alone; that I needed to believe that there is some energy greater than myself (the "they" of the first line of the poem), whom I could call on for support. You can call this God, creation, source, or whatever works for you.

Then I had a life-changing mystical encounter. It was during my long-term leave from my work as I was recovering from the illness, and I decided to surprise my son by driving four hours to see him. He was in college then and it was his birthday. The trip was wonderful and we had a great time. On my way home, I was lost in thought and music (rather loud music) as I was driving on the highway and reflecting on the sweet connection I had with my son. I was about to pull out to pass the car in front of me when I felt this massive push on my shoulder, which forced me back into my own lane. I then immediately saw a red car out of the corner of my eye that had been in my blind spot. We both were going very fast, and there was a solid cement median on our left. I was stunned—I was alone in the car; if that pressure/hand/whatever it was hadn't pushed me back, both I and the person in the red car would have been killed.

I could feel this presence on my shoulder for about a half hour and finally came to the realization that it had to be an angel or some form of spirit guide who had intervened and saved my life. There was no one in the car but me and there didn't seem to be any other explanation.

This was a huge turning point for me and I became fascinated with the mystical side of life. I know that there is way more than I understand and maybe will ever understand in this world, but I trust this support, and my once-cynical self turned to seek guidance and direction for my life from this mystical force. Now twenty years later, this part sometimes seems more real than the physical human body that I reside in. Having the awareness to see beyond what is visible has brought many precious gifts into my life and I love these experiences.

A more recent experience that was also a turning point came two summers ago. A couple of friends and I decided to take a sailing trip with a local sailor who gathered people together to experience the peacefulness of being on the water. We were doing a guided meditation and I was drawn to go to another part of the boat to do my own mediation. All of a sudden I saw this nun with a very specific habit (it had a white curl at the top of the headdress) and she was dressed in white. As I have said, I am not religious, so this seemed like an unusual image for me to have. The vision was so clear and it had a clear message: "I have come to teach you and give you an olive branch of peace". Yes, her name was Olive.

I listened as she shared that I was to take the crystal she offered and place it in my heart and it would activate the perfection that I already was. Crystals are part of nature and perfect in their creation. There is no limitation and this can be our experience as well when we trust the greater expression of ourselves. I was overcome with emotion and then she was gone. The feelings that were associated with this vision were very profound feelings of love, wholeness and a sense of perfection.

The gist of this teaching was that we are perfections of creation and the crystal was a mirror of this perfection. We just need to place this knowledge in our heart and ask anything that does not match this vibration to leave us. It sounded rather simplistic, but it really resonated with me and I still on occasion practise visioning this crystal and placing it in my heart and asking anything that does not match this vibration to leave my energy field. After that experience, Olive returned on many occasions and each time she had a teaching for me.

What was interesting is after this interaction I kept hearing about "zero point energy", which is the energy of the source or God, or whatever you want to call it. The term kept popping up everywhere and this is exactly what Olive was conveying to me: that the template of perfection is within ourselves (activated by this crystal when I placed it in my heart centre), and it is such a powerful magnetic force that all that doesn't belong has to leave.

Olive no longer seems to grace me with her presence, but I have assumed that the teaching was done and it was time for her to go.

I find that being tuned in to the mystical is a part of my everyday experience. I call upon these wonderful angelic or spirit forces to help and guide me. I even have my eight-year-old grandson sending ahead for parking angels, angels to create the right spot for us to park, when we go on our adventures together, and sure enough, a parking spot becomes available just when we need it. Life continues to get more and more amazing.

More recently I have become aware of a "benevolent being," which I lovingly call BB, who has come to make me aware of her/his presence. I have been informed that she has always been with me. It is so comforting to ask questions and have them answered and know that I do not have to do it all on my own, that support is available if I just ask for it. I am remembering to ask more often and am always so amazed at the results. Just a few months ago I was on a flight that arrived in my home town very late. I was tired and my car had been acting up by not starting. I assumed that it needed a new starter but I just hadn't had the time to take it in for servicing. There I was in the car after a thirteen-hour day, exhausted, and my car wouldn't start. I looked around the parking lot to see if anyone was around to help, but everyone had already left. I got into the car again and said, very forcefully, directing my focus to my unseen support team, "Start this car now—I am tired and I have to get home." I turned the key and the engine instantly started. I love these experiences—they are just further confirmation that there is unseen help when I just ask.

I am going to digress here a little. As my editor was commenting on my writing, she noticed that a lot of my stories take place around a car. I laughed, because she was right. There was a very good reason for this. When I was younger, I felt very powerless. I had a very dominating Mom who took a lot of her own anger and resentment out on me. I was a mirror for her to project all her sadness and disillusionment about life. This projection was quite often in the form of physical abuse. When I turned sixteen, I learned to drive a car and my Dad allowed me to borrow his quite often. Wow! Speeding along the highway all on my own gave me such a sense of power. You guessed it: I had a very heavy foot. I had dreams of becoming a race car driver! This was a power I had never felt before. From then on, cars represented power in my subconscious.

I first realized this truth when I was living on my own after my twenty-two-year marriage had ended. I was devastated. My whole life had turned upside down in a two-week period and the only thing that remained the same was the car I was driving. Job, home, city, everything was different. I kept perseverating about my car breaking down and I was almost in a panic that any minute some catastrophe was going to happen to the car I loved. When I sat with this and reflected on it, a light bulb went on and I realized that once again I felt powerless, and it wasn't that I was actually worried about my car breaking down; what was really going on was that I was terrified because I felt powerless again. That was quite an aha! moment. Once I realized this, the worrying stopped and I knew that my journey was to go within to that divine essence and connect to that place where we all are powerful.

Self-Awareness

The first thing to cultivate on the path of getting out of your own way is to create an acute self-awareness. Be the observer, and pay attention to the present moment. Bring your mind and ears to the now. Start savouring the information you perceive in the present moment. The more aware you become, the more you develop this skill until it's just running there in the background all the time. From this viewpoint, you can witness what you are experiencing. You'll become acutely aware of when the ego is on its rampage and whether you are in your hero or your thief mode; of whether you're bleeding or receiving. Without this self-awareness, you are unconscious and disconnected from your spirit and Divine intelligence. When you are conscious and open to life and in tune with your inner world, you can then become the director of your own life and choose what you want to experience. From this open, conscious place, you can tap into mystical realms offering you easier access to Divine intelligence.

Here are some helpful tips on self-awareness:

1. **Acknowledge what's going on**. Try not to gloss over it, put it out of your mind, or move on to the next thing. Instead, bring mindfulness to the moment, at whatever point you can, whether at the peak of your feelings or sometime later when you realize something significant has happened. Realize that you are preoccupied, or you're overreacting, or you did or said something inappropriate.

2. **Be open to your feelings**. Use a mindful awareness to explore the feelings connected with the episode that are strongest in you right now. Different patterns have distinctive emotional flavours: abandonment triggers anxiety; mistrust elicits rage; deprivation can foster a deep sadness. What are you feeling right now? Have you had similar feelings during past episodes?

3. **Notice your thoughts**. What are you thinking? What are you telling yourself about what happened, what you did or said? How do your thoughts try to justify what you did?

4. **What does this remind you of?** Have you had similar episodes to this one? Does this remind you of any episodes or feelings from your early years?

5. **Look for a pattern**. Can you see some consistency with other times you've had similar reactions?

Using Transformer 9—Positive Position or Transformer 2—Meditation will help to get you into the moment and release all the static in your mind so you can just focus on the Now.

There is more to self-awareness than just recognizing when something isn't working for us or where we are stuck. I think our gentle self needs to come into play here and we need also to be aware of the huge strides we have made on our journey. We are quite ready to notice our foibles, but we need to put immense energy into noticing our strengths! We must acknowledge where we have moved forward in our lives and congratulate ourselves on our progress. If there is a situation where before you may have reacted in a negative way and this time you didn't—you can acknowledge it by saying, "Wow. I didn't react to that—that's fantastic!" Celebrate this positive change and be aware of how far you have come.

In the past, anger was a huge trigger for me. When I was a child it usually had dire consequences. Interestingly, I picked social work as my field and it was a gold mine for the expression of anger. I knew intensely that I had to change this trigger so that anger didn't send me into such a debilitating place. I did many of the transformers in this book and worked intently to release this old fear in my subconscious. One day, a while back, I was with a friend and he was having an argument with his son and I realized my typical reaction would have been to go into fear; but I reminded myself, this has nothing to do with me, and I just didn't react. It was huge and I realized how much I had let go of and celebrated this.

What Is Your Inner World Like?

Now, ask yourself this: what is my inner space (my inner sensations like feelings and emotions and my physical state) made of? Have you ever done a little inner walk through your body? Is it a comfortable and calm place for you to reside, or is there often a storm brewing on the horizon? What does your inner energy feel like? Are you holding onto old resentments or hanging onto issues from the past?

Are you still ticked off at something that someone said or did? How does it feel hanging on to this baggage?

Hanging onto old stuff takes up precious room. Old stuff actually is stored in the body and takes up actual space. It's like having a room full of stuff that leaves no room for anything new to come in. The more space you use to contain this old stuff the less space there is for miracles, magic, and joy. How would your life change if you freed up space inside for something new?

I had a client a long time ago who had kept an enormous secret all her life. During our work together it became evident that this secret was taking up enormous space and energy and was part of her compulsive overeating. We often overeat to cover up our feelings and help us avoid what is really going on. Her "sister" was actually her daughter whom she had had when she was sixteen. She had kept this quiet and told no one. One day she decided that it was time. I could tell as soon as she came into my office that she had released this secret and had finally been honest. It was amazing to see the change in her. It took tremendous courage, but freed up so much inner space that she could now focus on other things, and her happiness quotient increased dramatically!

Are there people or events that have happened in your life that are taking up precious inner space? Do you spend time processing these relationships or events. Do they take up space in your head? People can be mirrors of our own baggage, but sometimes it also means that it is time to move on.

I had an amazing woman in my life to whom I felt extremely connected, even though we were very different women and very different in how we viewed friendships. I had an enormous love for this person; however, I found I was spending far too much inner space and energy processing this friendship. I felt constantly emotionally triggered and would have to process these emotions. As painful as it was, it was time to let this friendship go. Sometimes, we just need to let some friendships go. I did it kindly and with total honesty taking one-hundred percent responsibility for this choice. It was amazing how much space it freed up. Once I let this go, in flooded wonderful new friends with whom I have a loving and easy connection.

The Invitation, a poem by author and poet Oriah Mountain Dreamer, says this so succinctly:

"I want to know if you can disappoint another to be true to yourself,

If you can bear the accusation of betrayal and not betray your own self".

Get a piece of paper or your journal and create a list of what or who you are holding onto. Be brutally honest with yourself. Once you have the list, make a conscious intention that you are willing to let this go, not just some of it, but all of it. Many of the Transformers that I offer in this book are wonderful ways of releasing this old baggage. To find the best one, just pick the page in the transformer section that you feel speaks to you. One of the options can be Transformer 10—Materialize and Dematerialize. This can work well with the letting go and releasing of old baggage.

Think of all the inner space you can create with releasing all the old that doesn't fit for you anymore. What would your life be like? What could you do with all the space you free up? What kind of miracles can you then manifest?

Ho'oponopono

A while back, I took a course on the Hawaiian healing modality, Ho'oponopono, with Dr. Ihaleakala Hew Len, its recent proponent. Dr. Len is a psychologist in Hawaii who worked for a while in a mental health facility. He was a wonderful inspiration around cleaning up old stuff. He felt that we are all full of the collective ancient mind and that all we need to do is clean up our minds. He felt that what is in front of us—for example, someone expressing anger or aggression—is also within us, and that we are all capable of the worst and the best in behaviour. This premise is quite radical, but when you see the results that he had in his work at the facility, it certainly was compelling proof that ho'oponopono can have dramatic effects. He spent only a few years in this facility, and just "cleaned" anything that came in front of him. He would look at the files of the criminally insane patients in the mental health facility where he worked and recite this message: "I am sorry for the erroneous thoughts that have created this; please forgive me; thank you; I love you"; and other techniques used in Ho'oponopono.

Within a few years, most of the patients had left, because they no longer exhibited their old behaviours and therefore were able to return to the community. His story is quite amazing and you can find out more about it in Joe Vitale and Dr. Ihaleakala Hew Len's book, *Zero Limits*, and on their official website: www.zerolimits.info.

Be vigilant about judging yourself and others. If you find yourself judging, immediately shift gears and stop. Using a line from ho'oponopono will help enormously. Saying "I am sorry for the erroneous thoughts that have created this judgment. Please forgive me, I thank you, I love you", is a powerful way to get out of judging and back into flow. Judgment just creates negative space and is a major way we get in our own way. This has been a powerful tool for me and one that I use constantly to get out of judgement. It always brings me back to a peaceful place. See Transformer 8—Ho'oponopono in Chapter 11 for some of the tools and techniques.

When you create an inner climate from where you can cultivate inner peace, it in turn boosts your entire immune system, allowing you to live a longer, healthier life and to have more room for miracles. Ease is more effective than struggle to obtain what you want. People with relaxed attitudes accomplish much more than those in a state of fearful stress or agitation.

A Native American grandfather was talking to his grandson about how he felt after a tragedy. He said, "I feel as if I have two wolves fighting in my heart. One wolf is the vengeful, angry, violent one. The other wolf is the loving, compassionate one." The grandson asks him which wolf will win the fight in his heart. The grandfather answered, "The one you feed." In short, what you give energy to, thrives; what you don't, dissipates.

Schemas

When I first started doing my own healing work, I read *Emotional Alchemy* (Harmony Books, The Crown Publishing Group, 2002) by author and psychotherapist, Tara Bennett-Goleman. This had a huge impact on my own healing and later in the work I was doing with clients. It really helped to clarify where a lot of our BS comes from. For those reasons, I would like to paraphrase some of her work.

Bennett-Goleman classifies our personality patterns into what she calls "schemas". There are two groups of schemas: how we relate in close relationships and how we relate to the world. Her examples of schemas in close relationships are abandonment, deprivation, subjugation, mistrust, and unlovability; I have also seen a pattern of engulfment.

The abandonment schema can come from the loss of a parent or when a child loses a parent through divorce. The continuity isn't there anymore and they feel as though people who are supposed to be there to care for them leave; they feel abandoned. This feeling can also occur from frequent moves and never feeling really settled in one place. Deprivation can stem from physical or emotional abuse and neglect. Subjugation occurs when a child is totally controlled by an adult and feels they have no say in their lives. Mistrust is when their trust in their caregivers is breached and their needs are not met. The unlovability schema carries the feeling that a person is somehow flawed, leaving them wondering who would ever love them. Engulfment results in feeling suffocated by others. This could be from a smothering parent, in which emotions can skew energy boundaries. This schema can lead to a lack of commitment and a feeling of detachment.

Schemas that occur in the ways we relate to the world include exclusion, vulnerability, failure, perfectionism, and entitlement. Exclusion is when we feel left out and don't feel we belong, such as in school where there is an "in crowd" and you were on the outside looking in. Vulnerability is when you feel a loss of control and tend to awfulize that something bad is going to happen. Feeling fearful is a hallmark of this schema. The failure schema also has fear as its predominant emotion. The person feels they will never get it right and failure will always be the result. They are always "waiting for the next shoe to fall." In the perfectionism schema, the person feels they have to be perfect at all costs. This pattern can be exhausting; I found it to be very common. The person's sense of worth comes from having to get it right all the time. And finally, the entitlement schema occurs when a person feels entitled to whatever they want, whenever they want it, at another person's expense.

These schemas are underlying patterns that can be driving forces in our decisions and behaviours. They can come from parents, society, and information we have internalized early in our lives. They can be what is "driving our bus". Our schemas can limit our connection to our source and be limiting factors in how we conduct our lives. These patterns can be the major obstacles that get in our way. Awareness of these emotional patterns is key; releasing their hold through energy psychology or by using some of the Transformers can be life-altering. I have personally moved through many of these, as have many of my clients. The key to moving through them is having the awareness that they can be a driving force behind our behaviour.

I have found understanding these underlying patterns so helpful in recognizing what my triggers were. "Triggers" emotionally hijack a person quickly. For example, if your schema is unlovability and you are rejected by someone, the rejection can send you into a tail spin. If you are aware that that is just a pattern and not who you are, then you can change that pattern. Once you react and are aware why, you don't have to buy into the emotional schema and can then let it go much faster. It's hard to let old issues go, if you do not know they are there.

I saw how some of these patterns had a hold on my life by my reactions to my external world. "Exclusion" was a huge trigger for me. English is my second language and I only learned it when I went to school in Canada. My parents had just immigrated from Finland and I sure stuck out like a sore thumb at school: different hair, clothes, and no language to communicate with. My parents gravitated to the Finnish community and resisted taking on Canadian customs; I felt caught between two worlds: the one I was living in and the one my parents desperately clung to. I wasn't sure where I fitted in. It set up a pattern of feeling excluded for a good part of my life.

Releasing any of these patterns is so freeing; but first you have to know they are there.

Self-Value

Another important issue around your inner life is how you feel about yourself. How much value and self-respect do you own?

A long while back, I was teaching a course from my first book *Food and the Emotional Connection*, called "I'm Stressed—Pass the Chips". I had a young man in my class who had gone from an addiction to alcohol to an addiction to food. He just replaced one with the other. We talked about loving the self and self-valuing and I could feel he was very distressed about this concept. I asked him to share, and he said, "Isn't that being selfish? I have always been taught that was bad."

So we discussed the difference. Being selfish is an ego state in which you are putting yourself first at the expense of others. The dictionary describes this as "caring too much about oneself and not enough about others." Self-love on the other hand comes from the heart. It's about loving who we are so we can make choices that support ourselves. After some discussion he understood this and he had tears in his eyes because for the first time he allowed himself to value and love who he was. The whole class was quite moved by his story and it helped everyone to realize how much we need to love and value who we are. We have much more to give others when our own cup is full. When we come from a place of fullness within ourselves and give to others from this fullness, it always comes back.

Marc's is another story that shows this so clearly. Marc is a barber, a very unhappy barber, but he is also a wonderful painter with amazing artistic talent. His artwork is all over the living room floor; but that's as far as it gets.

What is stopping him from living his potential? It is a lack of self-value. Whenever you mention how wonderful his art is, he declines to accept the compliment. Our heart shrinks when we do not open to our potential. So, there sits his beautiful work all framed with nowhere to go, because Marc needs to see the value in himself before he can see the value in his work. Because his work is a true manifestation of what's inside him, he can't see its worth, because his worth is diminished in his own eyes.

When we feel good about ourselves and see our value and our magnificence, we can make choices that support this value. This in turn affects your choice of relationships, activities, the work you do, and how you nourish yourself. Every aspect of your life starts to measure up to your view of yourself. Your inner worth is determined by the externals in your life—only if you allow this to be true. We create our reality. Like my barber friend, if his self-value were to increase, if he could start to see his potential, value his talent, and say "I am worthwhile and my paintings are worthwhile," I have no doubt that they would be accepted and valued by buyers.

I think we are all looking for love, but need to provide this to ourselves first. We all want to know that we matter; it is human nature. The more we fill our own damaged pieces with love the more aligned we become one with the source that created us. Where we are crumpled up, we are a lie. When we unfold all the creases, we find out who we truly are: magnificence personified. Could the high incidence of heart disease have anything to do with being "heart sick" and not living our desires and dreams? Could this be related to feeling "bad" about ourselves, and constantly living within our limitations? We can be our own limiter or our own liberator. The choice is ours. We can choose to free ourselves from the constraints of limitation and liberate ourselves to think positively about ourselves and our future.

What kind of choices would you be making in your life if you loved and honoured yourself? What changes would you make? Are you also taking care of your own needs as you make choices about your work life, relationships, etc.? Are you nurturing your whole being?

List how you limit yourself. List ways you can liberate yourself. Make a commitment to choose the latter.

Poverty Consciousness

A major way I see how people limit themselves is around finances. Finances are such a reflection of how we feel about ourselves. Our self-value is so tied to this aspect of our external world. Lack of finances equals lack of self-value. The more we love and honour ourselves, the more we feel we deserve abundance in all its forms. I like to call this lack "poverty consciousness."

Poverty consciousness is that old tape that plays in your head: "money doesn't grow on trees", "there is never enough to go around". It's a feeling of a prevailing sense of "doom". I see this everywhere. You hear it in how people talk about money. Especially now in times of global financial meltdown, this seems to be on many people's minds. It is merely a perception of money that you may have attained from family or from ancestral history.

My family of origin was into poverty consciousness in a major way. I saw my parents struggle every day to maintain our basic life style. My Dad was 93-years old when he died and he was still "waiting for his ship to come in". A common line in our house was that my Dad was a man with rich ideas but a poor man's wallet. Both my parents had been brought up in Finland during the Finnish-Russian war in the late 1930s and struggling seemed to be very prominent in their lives. During most of my adult life, I too seemed to take this on. It was part of my patterns and probably one of the more challenging ones that I had to change.

Poverty consciousness is so damaging to our spirit and so unnecessary. There is abundance everywhere—it is just our stinking thinking that gets in the way of having it flow to us. Even if we are in difficult financial times, it is still up to us how we think about it.

For me personally, I feel so free of this past constraint that it doesn't matter what is going on in the global economy—I know that in my heart and mind I am abundant. If thoughts come in that say otherwise, I am quick to correct myself. I only have to look at what I have created to know that abundance is my true way of living in this world.

It has not always been that way, and in fact I had a financial crisis a while back that really made me dive into my shadow self and take a deep look at what I was carrying that wasn't even mine! Money issues can certainly bring on a dark night of the soul, but again it is just an opportunity to clean and clear the way for more abundance. Even in this dark time, I knew somehow I was being looked after.

This is how this dark night unfolded for me.

I have always loved the word "grace". To me it means a connection to my source and that magic is afoot. I love the song "Amazing Grace", and every time I hear the word I get tingles. During this difficult time I had made an appointment with a trustee office to get advice on the financial mess I was in. With a very heavy heart, I went for my first appointment. I sat down opposite this lady and she introduced herself, "My name is Grace." I almost started to laugh and felt such relief; I immediately knew she had an answer. Sure enough, she had a solution, which I had never even heard of, that would take me to total financial freedom in two years. I still smile when I remember hearing her name. Guidance is always available to us even in times of turmoil when we just listen and follow our instincts.

Changing these old patterns can lead you to so many opportunities that you would not otherwise welcome into your life. Once I felt more open around financial possibilities I decided that it was time to own a home again. I was on my own, self-employed, and older; I could see all the obstacles ahead. The mind loves seeing the obstacles. Plus, I had to release some old thinking about buying on my own—I quickly changed that thought pattern once I realized it was there.

I had visited a friend in a townhouse complex and thought *I could live here!* So I proceeded to decide first where in the complex I actually wanted to live, and made my choice. I then put flyers in everyone's mailbox and said I was looking for a private sale. I let everything go, left it up to the Universe, and just waited. About a month later, a woman called me from the section I had wanted to live in (an end unit to boot with no neighbours on one side—so desirable!) and said she was interested. She was moving into an apartment and since I was coming from an apartment, she was willing to leave me all the things I would need, like shovels, and all those kinds of things. I visited the place, and it was amazing. We came to a price, which was the price in my head, and it was a wonderful interaction. There were moments when I would fret about the few things that still needed to work out, but I quickly remembered that all was in order and I was just getting in the way. It all transpired beautifully and I moved into my new home a few months after.

The only thing that keeps us thinking small is our mind—move past your ideas of money and your limiting beliefs about it. Question every thought you have about money and get out of your own way and start creating abundance. It is everywhere and you too can create it.

What are your thoughts around money? Are you feeling deserving of lots of financial sustenance?

Chapter 3

The Mind: Ally or Foe

Messages from the Body

Our physical state is the mirror of our thoughts. "The body is the servant of the mind. It obeys the operations of the mind, whether they are deliberately chosen or automatically expressed. Disease and health like circumstances are rooted in thought. Strong, pure thoughts build up the body in vigor and grace," says James Allen.

Our body is constantly giving us messages that when heeded can lead us to make new choices that will support us. My illness was an example. It was a huge message. Some of us learn from inspiration and some from desperation. Desperation definitely forced me to go inside. Illness can just be a warning sign that not all is well with your world and something needs your attention. In my case it was a major "wake up call".

Start asking yourself questions. What message is your body trying to get across to you? What needs your attention?

Lila Dahl, in her book *Change Your Mind, Change Your Life*, talks about her experience of healing colon cancer after being given only two months to live, fifteen years prior to writing her book. Lila states: "Your reactions to your life experiences are based on the decisions stored in your cellular memory. Each organ stores particular emotions" (*Mind Revision*, 2002).

When I was sick, I spent enormous energy changing my diet and ensuring that what I put in my mouth would enhance my system. I took fistfuls of vitamins and herbal preparations and I was feeling better, but the change was slow and I felt like something was missing.

I found the missing link when I went inside to look at my emotional life. It was not a pretty sight.

Understanding our emotional makeup is crucial in healing physical symptoms, as they are so tied together. *Spontaneous Evolution* says it so clearly: "While the immune system is the guardian of our internal environment, the mind controls the immune system, which means the mind shapes the character of our health. . ." and "our mind control(s) our health and well-being as well as our diseases and our ability to overcome those diseases . . . Our mind shapes the character of our cellular community" (pages 15 and 16). Letting the mind with all its antics go unchecked has powerful implications.

Body Ailments and Their Emotional Correlations

I present these examples of body ailments and their emotional correlations as paraphrasing from Michael J. Lincoln, Ph.D.'s book *Messages from the Body*, as well as personal observations I have made during my practice. They are generalizations; everyone is unique and your emotional connection to your illness will also be unique. However, this will give you some idea of what could be going on inside.

Do any of these fit for you? Do you see anyone you know in these examples?

Backache

"Attack back". You are feeling a lack of emotional support from early on in life. You are over-responsible, and feel overloaded by all the excessive demands being made on you.

Bronchitis

Bronchitis refers to inflammation of the windpipe and bronchi. There is fear, tension, anxiety and a feeling of things being unsettled. When you are under stress or vulnerable, you feel that the world is not a safe place. You are suppressing grief. You are frustrated and angry with yourself, but are afraid to express or let go of it.

Cancer

You give too much to others and don't take care of yourself. You ignore your inner pain by attending continuously to others' needs to the detriment of the self. You engage in self-rejection. There is resentment, hurt, hopelessness, inner conflict, and a sense of powerlessness. There is also the feeling of being the long-suffering victim. You are a very loving, supportive person, but this loving energy needs to be turned in toward the self.

Cataracts

You are seeing a dark future ahead, in which there is no joy and no end in sight. You want to control your future and to impose your will, but you have not learned a way in which do that.

Cholesterol Problems

This is a "grin and bear it" orientation. Life feels like it is a problem to be solved and a very serious business indeed. The problem arises from a type of dysfunctional family where you had to maintain sanity and deflect disaster. You suffer from a lack of joy.

Chronic Fatigue Syndrome, Gland Problems, Meningitis

"Pooped out." You are pushing beyond your limits, and you have a dreaded fear of not being good enough. You were draining all of your inner support and a stress virus took hold. You are "running on empty," due to overwhelm and deprivation exhaustion.

Colds; "The Common Cold"

You need to take time out to handle the emotional and mental issues that are bothering you. The effect is a feeling that too much is going on and there is mental conflict that is causing confusion.

Colitis

Inflammation of the lower colon suggests that you feel insecure and have a difficult time letting go. You feel burdened and, at times, lonely. You tend to feel pessimistic and unloved.

Environmental Allergies

You are allergic to your environment, indeed to just about everything, and are completely blown out by your need for total hands-on control of everything. You simply have to take charge of the critical parameters of every situation. Your feeling is that if you don't, all hell will break loose. Yet, at the same time, you deny your own power and self-worth.

Flu

You have feelings of being under the influence of weakness and help-lessness. They may reflect the vulnerable feelings that accompany times and processes of great change. You have a strong experience of lack of support and protection.

Gall bladder problems

You are irritated with other people and the world around you, which results in stored up old anger.

Headaches

You are blocking the flow of life and somehow feel that you are wrong. You have anxiety about things that aren't handled—including your anger. Some circumstance, relationship, situation, issue, pressure, individual, or whatever it is that you dislike but which you feel you have to put up with or to live with is really bothering you.

Heart Problems

"Broken-hearted". You have little sense of personal worth or deserving-ness of love. It is a result of a dysfunctional family who gives you or gave you little support, nurturance, acceptance, or fulfillment.

Immune System Problems

You are harbouring deep grief and a sense of underlying despair. You are overwhelmed by too much sorrow, and by the "running on empty" effect of a severe inequality of energy exchange with the world, whereby you put out much more than you get. It is a result of having carried the world on your shoulders all your life.

Indigestion

"Stones in the stomach". The reality you are dealing with and taking in is causing you upset and disharmony with yourself. It is responsibility overload leading to tension, fear, and anxiety. You tend to push yourself and overwork.

Migraine Headache

Longing for love from someone close. You have an abiding fear of rejection and abandonment, in response to which you develop a perfectionistic compensation attempt—trying to "earn" your right to love. You drive yourself and you strive to get things done.

Neck Problems

Being rigid and inflexible and refusing to see other sides of a question. You are under a lot of stress.

Shoulder Problems

The shoulders reflect our feelings and thoughts about what we are doing and how we are doing it, as well as our attitudes about our responsibilities and how others are relating to us. Shoulders are the seats of responsibility, and difficulties here reflect feelings of being overburdened.

We think our negative thoughts, anger, frustration, are just thoughts, but they affect the total functioning of our whole body.

Other Messages

Understanding body ailments is one way we can receive messages from our spirit self, but there are numerous additional ways this energy tries to communicate with us.

Other more subtle ways are dreams. I have found that when I pay attention to my dreams, these internal messages can bring me such amazing gifts and make my life much easier.

A year before being diagnosed with a bladder-related disease, I had numerous dreams of overflowing toilets. I was getting pretty sick of these dreams. One morning after again having this recurring dream, I took action and wrote it all down. I had read a bit about dream analysis and thought, "Okay, it is time I figured this out."

I will never forget the day. It was in January 1994. I even remember where I was sitting. It was as though a huge light bulb went off and I realized the dream was about being "pissed off". Wow! What was I pissed off about? It was about too much responsibility, and again this stemmed back to my youth, when I had had to become a parental figure at a very early age. This realization was a pivotal point in my healing and I realized how strongly this emotional connection was tied to my disease. I began the task of unraveling my emotional baggage and making peace with my past. That is when I really started to get well. That was the turning point.

Another dream that had a profound effect on my life was during a time of crisis when I had just left my marriage. I was devastated and the grief was enormous. Every night for three nights, I cried and cried but at 5:00 a.m. each morning when I finally slept, I dreamed that I was flying, flying high in the sky with no effort, over hills and valleys and lakes. They were such freeing dreams. I knew that as painful as this decision to leave my marriage had been, the outcome of this choice was freedom! Not just freedom from a marriage, but freedom to become who I was really meant to be. If it hadn't been for those dreams, I am not sure if I could have kept going forward. I am very grateful for those dreams. Now, seventeen years later, my life is so full of freedom.

From then on, I paid very close attention to what my dreams were. If I was making a major decision about something, I would always sleep on it with the intention of remembering whatever I dreamed. If the dream was a negative one, then I knew I needed to make another choice. On one occasion a friend and I had thought about buying a house together. That night I dreamed we were in my car on a journey and we crashed. That was a pretty clear message and both of us agreed that it wasn't the right choice at that time.

A side note—if you have difficulty remembering your dreams, supplementing with a B6 vitamin can help.

Our higher selves, the wise parts of us that are connected to Divine Intelligence, are always trying to communicate with us. It can be through messages in the body or dreams, or sometimes you just get a knowing, an "aha!" and you know the truth. A "gut" feeling is also another way, when you just have a sense that something is right for you or not. Usually these are felt in the solar plexus area. I quite often get a rush of energy and I know some information I have picked up from the client or myself is worth paying attention to. How you receive messages will be unique to you. Make yourself familiar with how you receive these, and then pay attention and listen to your inner voice, to any nudges that you may have. Physical signs are strong indicators that you need to pay attention. Once you have this information, you can then make choices based on this intelligence and not on the ego-limited mind. Learning to stay tuned in to this voice is the "Journey of the Hero." Sometimes, we may not like what it says, but it will always take us to where we need to go.

The first step is to hear, but it may also require some action, like my example of the car crash dream. I listened to the dream and then made a choice to not go through with our plans to buy a house together. If I hadn't acted on this message, it most likely would have ended in a crash of some kind. Most of us have had the experience of recognizing a gut feeling about something and then not following through, only to say to ourselves, "Why didn't I listen?" I have been there, done that, many times, and now I listen and follow the guidance I receive and always stay open to receiving this support.

How do you receive messages from your wise self? Do you listen and pay attention and follow your guidance? If this is an area you need to work on, what could you do to be more in tune with your Divine Intelligence and innate wisdom? The transformer section can give you some tools to use that will support this inner journey.

How Clean Is Your Mind?

We think that our negative thoughts (anger, frustration) are just thoughts, but as I mentioned earlier, they affect the total functioning of our body. In the Energy Psychology classes I teach—I created the modality basing it on Applied Kinesiology—I ask people to hold up their arm and resist as I press down. This creates a muscle-strength basis from which to test—it is called muscle testing using an indicator muscle. I ask them to think about something positive. The muscle is strong and the arm stays up. Then I get them to think about a challenge in their lives and we go through the same process. The arm immediately drops, showing the negative thinking is having a weakening effect on the muscles in the body.

We store our stress in our cells and tissues. What if you are stressed all the time and constantly focusing on the challenges in your life? How do you think this is affecting your whole body?

Here is a little exercise for you to try. Sit in a chair. Raise one leg and press down on it, resisting at the same time. Think of something positive. Your leg should stay strong. Now change your thoughts to a challenge that you are facing. How does your leg test now? Is it as easy to keep it up? Typically, it is not.

You can also try this exercise with negative self-talk. How does your muscle react when you say something negative to yourself such as, "that was stupid?" Now, say something positive, "you are a warm and caring person." How does that feel?

In his book, *The Dragon Doesn't Live Here Anymore*, inspirational New Thought lecturer and author Allen Cohen says: "If you now have negative circumstances in your life, cease to dwell on them mentally, and they will leave you. The best way to get rid of an unwelcome guest who lingers at your home is to empty the refrigerator. He'll be forced to seek refuge elsewhere. When we stop feeding our bad habits and conditions with thought and feeling energy, they will drop off like an old scab. If we pull out the plug from an electromagnet, all of the scraps of junk metal that cling to it fall off instantly. Refuse to water a weed, and die it must. Negative circumstances cannot survive when we refuse to sustain them with emotional energy".

Simply put: great thoughts equal feeling great. Yucky thoughts equal feeling yucky. It's pretty simple, but not always easy to attain great thoughts. The mind can be very habitual and it will go to your default mode especially at times of stress. That's why the Transformers in this book are such wonderful tools. They can help you stay on track and keep your energy and mind clean.

When I was at the seminar with Dr. Len, the Hawaiian psychologist who teaches Ho'oponopono, his opening line was, "Have you noticed whenever you have a problem *you* are always there?"

We seem to see our problems as something happening to us, but we are part of them. We create them and we have a choice to un-create them or at least to look at them differently

Our egos love drama; drama gives ego power. The world is full of drama. Just tune into any reality TV shows and realize this is major "food for our egos". The more drama you are attracted to the more you create. So stop feeding the mind with reality TV shows and other forms of drama.

Have you noticed that when stuff starts to go wrong, it just feeds on itself and creates more. Yucky thoughts create more of the same and then draw to you more yuck. You lose your keys, you drop a container of juice, you swear at the chair that you just stubbed your toe on, and on and on it goes.

We incessantly talk about our problems at work or with our family and the more we do this the more drama we create.

Learn to get **bored** with your problems and they will get bored with you. Don't give them feeling energy. If you find you are with someone and they are going on and on—detach yourself; let your mind go to a peaceful place. Drama is exhausting. It puts a hold on your dreams and is an energy drain.

Another energy drain that creates drama is complaining. Whenever I am with someone who complains, I have to tune out or sometimes change the subject to something more neutral or positive and let go of the energy. If you find yourself complaining, make a choice to stop. Each negative thought is detracting you from a joyful easy life. Why go there? Focus instead on what could go right.

Simply put, we are undeniably responsible for our lives. Wed to this responsibility is the freedom to use the laws of life in whatever way we choose. We can create heaven or hell for ourselves through our thoughts and our actions. Do not wait for the world to stop "socking it to you". Start generating as many positive thoughts as you can, and you will bear witness to miraculous changes in your life. Think love, success, and happiness, and sooner or later these blessings are sure to be yours. Concentrate on that which you would become, not that which you now believe you are, and you will enter a new realm of consciousness—one of chosen good. The formula for ease is quite simple:

thoughts = how you feel

and

how you feel = what shows up in your life.

I know you have probably heard this many times before and your ego is probably saying, "Yeah—but it isn't that easy." That's why I have presented you with solutions: the Transformers at the end of this book. Use them to move past these blocks. It will make it easier to stay on track.

"When we search for happiness and an end to suffering the only place to look is within the mind itself. We each contain within ourselves all that we need for personal joy, bliss, wisdom, equanimity and peace. There is no reason to look to externals or anywhere else. When one truly embraces this thought, there is nothing to fear. We are truly free." Thus says spokesperson for Buddhism, Western-born Lama Surya Das in *Awakening the Buddhist Heart*, (page 189). Realizing this enables us to go to that quiet inner space, so we are not always at the mercy of the externals in our life.

Outer Versus Inner Technology

As a society, we have created a world where we focus on our outer technology. We have iPhones, Blackberries, computers, and every gadget you can imagine to make our lives "easier". But, are they making life easier? We are very proficient at creating diversions with new technology being created all the time. This outer technology certainly seems to rule our world. What would happen if all the wireless servers were down—it would certainly create mass chaos.

Technology has an amazing place in our lives and I am certainly glad that I recently joined the twenty-first century and got a smart-phone. This technology is very helpful when I have arrived at the wrong location to meet a friend and can call and find out where we were actually supposed to meet, or I'm running late and can let them know where I am. It is very useful. There are many forms of technology that can support our connecting.

However, I think this left-brain function contributes to the separateness that is the disease of our society. We are disconnected from one another and the true needs of our hearts and souls are being ignored. We communicate, but we do not really connect. Our hearts aren't open to each other. I watch people so engrossed in their technology that they are not present in their lives. They are so focused on this outer technology that the inner technology, which is our ability to tune in to ourselves and each other, to be present in our lives and connect spiritually in a deep way and to stay open to one another, is lost.

I watched a young man with his child. With one hand, he was playing with his daughter and in the other hand was his iPhone, which he was working on. Was he present to his daughter and fully engaged? I think not. She was only getting a fragment of his attention.

I saw another example of this in the Hong Kong airport when I walked past a mom with her five-year-old little boy sitting at a table in the restaurant. Her thumbs were going on her phone and he was doing exactly the same thing on a similar device. Both were engrossed in outer technology. He was five-years-old!

Recent studies have shown that constant and intense engagement with electronics is rewiring children's brains. Addiction is a real possibility. The gadgets need to be faster, more stimulating to get our attention and to keep people engaged. We are losing our ability to truly tune into ourselves and each other and recognize subtle energies from within ourselves and from others that can give us important messages.

However, when we focus on our inner technology, through meditation and many of the transformers that create this inner awareness, we allow for a much richer and more fulfilled life where we have easy access to higher wisdom. We are then tuned into our inner landscape and are aware of subtleties that are happening there, such as exactly how our body is feeling; if anything needs our attention. One is then also more in tune to messages that can come just out of nowhere and can have a huge impact on our lives.

I like to call these hugely impacting messages "downloads". Writing this book was one of those downloads. I had written one prior book and had no intention of doing another, and then one day, just as I was allowing myself to just be, with no music, no phone, and no outer technology, I got this message that it was time to write again. I tried to argue, but it was no use; the whole concept and title just landed. This has happened on numerous occasions. I allow myself to stay open by limiting the outer technology and staying tuned in to my inner technology. It also helps us tune in to each other and recognize others' energies—whether they need our attention.

Outer technology can leave us in our own world and not tuned in to the people around us.

I also think the by-product of focusing on inner technology is that I feel I am always safe. I am tuned into the present moment and allowing myself to totally engage in whatever I am doing. So I know if something isn't right, and if I get an intuitive sense to react in some way, I am open to it. How many accidents occur because people are engaged in outer technology and not staying tuned in to their lives?

There was a very sad case in my province in Canada where a young man with earphones on had tuned out both his outer world and his inner signals and was walking on the street when a plane crashed on him and he was killed. He had no idea this was happening, because he was too busy with outer technology. This is an extreme example, but it did happen. If he had been more engaged in his surroundings, he would have easily seen and heard the imminent danger.

I see this disconnect so much with younger people: they can be in a van with five other people who know each other and all are in their own worlds, disconnected from each other even though they are sitting right beside each other. There is no eye contact; instead there is a sense of isolation.

As I have mentioned, my country of origin is Finland where cell phones and smart-phones are everywhere—even my auntie who is ninety has her own. Again, don't get me wrong—it is very handy and I would not be without my smart-phone, but I watch as people walk down the street, everyone with some appendage attached to their ears. No one is making eye contact or engaging with each other. They are all just engrossed in their own microcosm. Nowadays, we don't even talk to each other, we text.

Recently, I was having a discussion about this with a friend and her comment was, "I think people hide behind this way of communication." I tend to agree.

I think a lot of it is an intimacy avoidance. We don't have to truly connect and can stay safe without feeling vulnerable. Texting and emailing can also cause huge miscommunication that is much less likely when you are face to face and are able to really understand what the other person is trying to communicate. It is well accepted that 80 percent or more of our communication is non-verbal, through gestures, facial expressions, and tone of voice.

Even worse is what outer technology is doing to young people. Many don't have the social skills necessary to function in the world as human beings, because their idea of reality is skewed from television, video games, and a barrage of media misinformation.

I witnessed another example of people focusing on outer technology at a retreat. The workshop leader was constantly taking pictures, even when there was a spiritual ceremony. I realize she wanted to capture these moments, but she was missing the experience of being there herself and really feeling what was happening. She only witnessed it through the lens of a camera. She will have mementos of the event, but she will be missing the memories.

I also think that technology is a distraction that we have created to keep our pain at bay. It allows us an escape from our inner world, and keeps us from connecting with our own truth. The ego loves distractions. I have a friend who always says he is so busy, so busy with technology that it keeps him from going inside to see how he really feels and what's really going on for him. Technology numbs us to our inner world and inhibits us from truly engaging in our own lives.

A long while ago, my then-husband and I and our three young children had an amazing opportunity to live in Germany for three years. This was in the late 1970s and early 1980s. There were no phones where we moved to: TV was only in German and the VCR was just being created. We had to interact with each other. I think it was the most wonderful time our family had. We would sit together and talk and make tapes where the kids would sing songs or tell stories to the grandparents. This was a form of technology, but we were all engaged with each other together as we were doing this, and the benefit to the grandparents was enormous. We would sit at the table for long periods and sing and just interact. Our kids would play outside and with each other and were very creative in their activities, even climbing the church steeple (without our knowing, of course!). They played and were active and had fun without any outer technology. Life was so spontaneous; people would just show up, since no one had a phone. The support in this community was something I will always remember.

Being tuned in to our inner technology allows us to be open to our existence as a whole: tuning in to our neighbours and friends and, most of all, tuning in to yourself and others, being so self-aware that you can sense your surroundings and listen to what is right for you. You may see two paths in front of you and you will have the inner knowing as to which is the right one. You can tune in to your friends or family and know when they need your support.

When I first started doing energy work and tuning into my clients—work such as energy psychology or the two pointing system, which is also called Matrix Energetics—I was amazed at what I was able to pick up from their energy. When they verbalized how they were feeling, it was always exactly what I was picking up. Now I know that science labels this "quantum entanglement," which is a fusion of energies, where you literally become one with the other person, where you become one with their energy.

When we are tuned in to our inner technology we are open to all of life in the physical and mystical, and it can truly create some amazing experiences.

The more I was able to get out of my own way and tune in to my inner technology, the more mystical and magical my life became.

Turn the Channel to a New Station

Start changing the channel and start tuning into your inner world and the channel of the heart. Use any of the tools that help you focus inward, like meditation and deep breathing. Whenever you feel your mind has taken hold and you are running amok with thoughts, take a moment to just drop into your heart (see Transformer 11—Three Heart Energy Exercises). "Dropping into your heart" means taking the focus away from the mind and moving your focus to the heart area. Really feel what it is like to be in this place.

Saying affirmations is also a good way to change the channel and get heart-focused, but affirmations without feelings are just empty words. The key with affirmations is not just in saying them, but adding feeling energy to them. If your affirmation is about self-value, feel what it is like to be valued. If this is difficult, search for memory for a time when you felt valued and go back to this feeling. I find thinking about my grandchildren always evokes feelings of love and caring. It makes my heart feel warm and then I transfer this feeling to myself or to the situation.

You can also use Transformer 9—Positive Position when saying your affirmation. This can further help to dislodge the negative and give more energy to your new positive thoughts. Your whole physical state will respond and the psyche will be much more receptive to your new thoughts about yourself. Feeling energy is emotion, and emotion when positive can have a powerful effect on your whole physical system including the immune system. It will energize your life force.

Chapter 4

Make Your Energy Work for You

How is Your Energy Affecting Your World and the People around You?

I am sure you have had the experience of walking into a room and immediately noticing that something is off. I quite often take a step back when I feel this uncomfortable energy. Everything is energy and we are picking up the energy around us all the time and sharing our energy with others without even knowing it.

When I first began this journey, I read that if you heal yourself it will heal those around you. I was pretty skeptical and couldn't quite understand how this would possibly work. Then I had a vivid example of this and became a believer.

I had a very challenging relationship with my mother as I have stated, one that drained my energy at every turn. My parents lived near me at the time of this experience I am going to share. They were quite elderly and needed lots of my support. But, boy, did I resent it! I knew I had to heal this too in order to move forward. What I wasn't expecting was the effect this healing would have on my mother. One day I was at her home for her eightieth birthday and by this time I had cultivated a very peaceful heart around my Mom. This had not been an easy task, but I was grateful that here I was in my fifties, and I had finally managed to overcome my resentment and forgive. I was sitting next to my Mom and, for some reason, I put my head on her lap. This type of affection had never occurred before and, to my amazement, she started stroking my hair and was so gentle and kind. My tears just poured and I silently cried, for this was the first time in my life that I had experienced this type of emotion and loving energy from my Mom. Healing had occurred for both of us. I was amazed!

Another more recent experience shows how interconnected we all are, and this happened while at work. I am a flight attendant, and I was at the front of the airplane, greeting our guests as they came aboard my flight. I could feel a calm, peaceful energy approaching me, even before I saw a monk in his full robes coming down the bridge. I could feel this amazing, peaceful energy emanating from him, and I smiled and said, "I am glad you are here—it should be a quiet peaceful flight." He just smiled. Later, we had a nice interaction and again I could feel a beautiful, calming energy emanating from him. Yes, the long flight home was calm and even the call light that usually goes on quite often did not go on once!

Affecting our surroundings isn't just about positive thinking and positive attitude, though these are extremely important. It is about positive "being". We need to BE that peaceful, calm energy, so it fills up the space all around us and has a calming effect on all whom we come into contact with in our energy field.

Parents will be amazed to see how strongly this impacts their children. When you are the centre of calm and peacefulness, your children also become calm and peaceful. When you are chaotic, stressed, and anxious, your children suddenly become wild, chaotic, and unruly! It's the energy you're giving off, and they're like absorbing little sponges. So, if you want your children to calm down, be peaceful, and quiet, try taking some time to make sure you're giving off the right energy.

What is Energy/Chi?

You can't see it or smell energy/chi, but you can feel it. Eastern philosophy believes this is actually our life force. We are all energy beings and this force within us can be a strong determinant on how we are feeling and operating in our world.

You may be very familiar with this force of energy, or this may be a relatively new concept for you. If it is the latter, you may want to try this little exercise. Place your hands, palms facing, opposite each other about six inches apart. Now move them further apart and then closer together. Put your focus on the space between your hands. What do you feel? Most people feel a sense of tingling or warmth. What you are feeling is energy, also known as chi, the pulsating force of our lives.

When our energy is flowing freely this brings harmony and balance to our lives. Blocks in our energy flow, however, from poor eating habits to old traumas, memories, and all the old baggage we carry, can lead to limiting patterns and even illness that stop us from realizing our true potential and the peace that we all have inside of us.

We are all energy beings and as mentioned earlier when we are in other people's energy, we are in quantum entanglement, which is a merging of our energy field with another. I am sure you have had the experience of being near someone who is not in a good space and you start to feel that as well, or the opposite, someone is very happy and peaceful, and you start to feel that way. You are picking up on their energy.

Susan was visiting Mary (not their real names); as Susan had been diagnosed with cancer, Mary asked if I could do some energy work on her. As I entered Susan's energy field and experienced quantum entanglement, I was drawn far into her energy field. There I felt a tremendous pain; it hurt to be in contact with it; it was something very painful; I could hardly stand to connect with this energy. I asked Susan what she was holding onto. She shared that her granddaughter had been murdered. There was huge pain around this; plus, Susan was in a very unhappy marriage. Her energy alone told a huge story, which was all recorded in her energy field and took up enormous space for her to carry around in her physical body. It had become so enormous that her body was literally attacking itself, manifesting as cancer. Susan also fit the classic personality of someone who takes care of everyone else and not herself.

Traumas such as these, which can have such a destructive effect on our physical bodies, can be palpable; paying attention to them and releasing them can be lifesaving.

Reading energy is fascinating to me. There is so much held in our information energy that when tapped into can be so enlightening. I had one situation with a client that was such a clear example of how we can pick up on what others are experiencing.

This person was going to court for the organization he was working for, to testify regarding a fellow colleague. This person was quite upset and nervous about this impending experience. As I was holding acupressure points to release some of his tension, I began to feel a choking sensation and could hardly breathe. I asked, "What you are thinking about!" And he said, "I want to strangle the guy." I asked him to change his thoughts!

We are constantly engaged in interpreting the world around us. When we are in proximity and especially when we are in close proximity with others, we can be picking up stuff that isn't even ours. The more peaceful you are inside, the easier it is to filter out what doesn't belong to you, allowing you to keep your energy clean and clear.

What Inhibits the Flow of Energy/Chi?

When our energy is flowing easily we are in harmony with all of life and the life force that created us. Keeping our bodies and environments free of pollution and distorted energies helps to keep our own energy clear. **Everything** affects our energy, from external sources to our internal environment. External sources of distortion can be pollution, cleaning fluids, EMFs (electromagnetic fields), cell phones, laptops, other people's negative or positive energies, clothing we wear, such as underwire bras, and body adornments such as belly rings, especially in the hara (a Japanese term referring to the energy centre around the belly button).

In his book *Biology of Belief,* leading-edge research scientist Bruce Lipton, Ph.D., says our environment controls our cells: "The distribution of electromagnetic charge within a cell can be altered by interference from electromagnetic fields such as those emanating from cell phones." I look forward to scientific research verifying this claim.

As I mentioned earlier, I do an interesting exercise with students in my Energy Psychology classes. I muscle test their arm and it is strong. Then I get them to hold a cell phone in the other hand and test again and the arm is weak. I have them put the cell phone down and again their arm is strong. You can do this with anything: foods that you are allergic to, metal, or any other electronic device; even some people can elicit this reaction.

Our internal environment also has a profound effect on our energy. This can include our own negative thoughts, poor nutrition, drugs, and alcohol. The list goes on and on. I do a similar exercise with students and their thoughts. I will again muscle test to ensure I have a strong muscle, then ask the person to think about something they love. I test the arm and of course it is very strong. I ask them then to think about something or someone who is challenging to them, and again the arm goes weak.

Sometimes observers in the group can witness the total physical effect. The subject's shoulders droop, their head comes down, and they may frown. Their whole physical structure is affected by just a thought. If that isn't motivation to keep your mind clean, I don't know what is!

Be cognisant of how your inner and outer environments are affecting you. Being vigilant will motivate you to make better choices so that you will keep your energy clear and clean.

Sometimes others will project their "stuff" upon you, but you always have the choice of whether to receive this or return to sender. We have an internal sense of well-being that is not dependent upon the externals of our lives, but that comes from deep within us. When we can remain in that centre, like being in the eye in the storm, chaos can occur around us, but we do not need to give feeling energy to this chaos. The more you are in tune with your "God Self," the less you are affected by others and what's going on around you.

Just think what would happen if you believed that you could be happy for no reason at all! How would that change your life?

I had a personal example of this that made me realize how grateful I am for my inner peace, my internal well-being. I was walking down a street in Bangkok, which is a very chaotic city where the pollution from vehicle emissions is extraordinarily high. My nose felt like it was burning from simply breathing the air. As I was walking, just noticing all the noise and frantic energy around me, I could feel an immense peace inside, and thought, "Wow. I have come such a long way that I can feel this powerful stillness and inner peace in the midst of such chaos." It was an extraordinary moment.

Keeping your Energy Clean

Since the early 1990s when I healed my illness, I have been fascinated with energy and how it affects our bodies. When I first started training in the energy work that is known as Health Kinesiology and also known as Energy Psychology, I was going through a very challenging separation from my then-partner; I couldn't stop perseverating about the problem: I was obsessing; the separation was totally consuming my life. While training in an energy class, the instructor used me as a model and I took the opportunity to focus on this issue. We went through the process (we call them "corrections") and when we were done, it was as though someone had kindly taken the problem totally away and said, "You don't need this anymore", leaving me feeling at ease and peaceful. I was amazed and stunned at how I could feel so different, in just a matter of minutes. I became totally committed to helping others to change their circumstances by changing and cleaning their energy.

The reason I think it is so critical for us to clean our energy is that all our "stuff" is located in our cells and tissues, not in the brain, and clearing this energy has a powerful effect on our whole bodies that frees us. We know this is true from Dr. Candace Pert's work in the field of pharmacology. In the 1990s, she discovered that the body, not the brain, is the subconscious mind and that it communicates via neuropeptides, molecules that are produced by every thought we have. Dr. Pert discovered that thoughts have a biochemical component: "While thoughts are real, neuropeptides are real and the brain is real; what we think of as the mind is actually the ego in disguise" (Alberto Villoldo, Ph.D., *The Four Insights*, page 164).

We spend so much time cleaning our homes, our cars, and our physical bodies; yet most people ignore cleaning their energy, which is the very life force that supports us. We are magnets for all kinds of energy, as mentioned above, and we are constantly in a soup of energetic information, which quite often sticks to us. So making a regular habit of cleaning your energy/chi just makes so much sense. Keeping your energy clean will also have an influence on keeping your consciousness in a cleaner state. It's all interconnected.

Give the Universe Clear Directions

The Transformers in Chapter 11 are excellent ways to clean your energy and keep it clean. It does take practise and some consistency to do this on a regular basis; however, the payoffs are enormous. I have been practising keeping my energy clean since my illness over twenty years ago, and I know that this is the main reason I am in such a peaceful place in my life where manifesting what I desire has become fairly easy. The Universe needs instructions so it can give us what we desire. I make a regular habit of doing some form of clearing every morning and setting a clear intention of how I want my day to unfold. This routine usually also includes a meditation. My practice varies and sometimes it is shorter and sometimes longer, depending on what my day looks like.

Setting clear intentions on how you want to experience your day and doing some form of centring or energy-clearing exercise will reap enormous benefits for your day. Even if you can only afford five minutes, do whatever you can manage. It may take a while to play with the Transformers to see what works for you. Be intuitive and playful about your choices; it will be easier to stick with them. And if some days you just don't feel like it, go with that as well. If you have difficulty picking a routine, then just intuitively pick a page from Chapter 11. Doing this for yourself is a powerful way of saying you value and love yourself and you are worthy of taking time for YOU.

When you are feeling stuck or not in a good space then doing some of these Transformers is a powerful way of changing your energy patterns so you can get out of your way and connect to your inner wisdom. This will help you get back into a peaceful place much more quickly. Another way I have found to clean stuck energy that seems so simple, but really works, is just to shake it off. If you need to, put some music on and just shake all over. I know this may sound kind of silly, but it really works. It's even an idiom in our language that when something bugs or hurts you, "just shake it off". I have found that when I work with clients when the energy moves, there is quite often an involuntary body movement, which is an indicator that energy has shifted. Quite often when I meditate, if something is stuck, my body just shakes and I know something is working its way out; I feel much clearer after. The shaking helps the energy move and release.

What We Put in Our Mouths

Everything in our lives affects our energy and one major component is what we put in our mouths. This affects every cell in our body and whether we are feel vitality or lethargy. A knowledge of wholesome nutrition is my background and eating high quality, vibrant food along with releasing negative thinking had a huge role in my overcoming my illness.

For more information on healing with nutrition, see my book *Food and the Emotional Connection*.

What we eat is assimilated into our body and is the fuel that it has to work with. If your diet is full of vibrant whole foods then your energy is whole and vibrant. If not and it is full of toxins, then your energy is toxic and the body has to work harder to maintain its balance. For example, diets high in sugar suppress the immune system and leave a person much more susceptible to illness. Just like naturopathic doctors, I have always maintained that an illness is not about the germs we have, but whether we are a friendly host for those germs or not.

Without getting into great detail regarding nutrition, I include a quick little assessment tool for you to see where you are. Putting some energy into giving your body high quality fuel will go a long way toward helping you keep your energy in a vibrant and healthy state.

Nutritional Assessment: Are You Eating For Vitality and Peak Performance?

Please score a number "1" beside the statement that applies to you, then total each column.

- I drink coffee in the morning as a way of starting my day.
- I eat fast food once per week.
- I eat fast food more than once a week.
- I buy packaged food regularly.
- I eat snacks like chips and cheezies while watching TV or as a treat more than once per week.
- I feel tired around two to three o'clock in the afternoon.
- I drink the occasional soft drink.
- I drink soft drinks regularly (at least once a day).
- I never eat fish.
- I eat sugared cereal in the morning.
- My typical breakfast is coffee and a muffin or donut.
- I drink very little water, no more than one glass per day.
- I regularly feel fatigued.
- I eat red meat on a regular basis, more than once per week.

- I buy and eat canned vegetables.
- I love lots of processed or concentrated fruit juices.
- I eat sugary items like cookies, muffins, donuts, and sweet snacks at least once each day.
- I occasionally read labels, but typically just buy what I like.
- I never read labels and just shop for items I like.
- I eat fried foods on a regular basis (more than once per week).
- I give little thought to the way I eat and tend to eat unconsciously.
- I never take any supplements.
- I know my health is being affected by the food choices I make, but find it very difficult to make any changes.
- I eat mainly white bread with the occasional whole wheat, but this is in the regular sandwich-bread form.
- I use bread a lot in my daily diet (at least twice a day).

Total Score:_____

Choosing to steer clear of the above activities is a choice in the right direction toward optimal health!

- I typically shop the periphery of the grocery store: the vegetable, dairy, and meat sections.
- I drink at least four to five glasses of water a day.
- I drink eight glasses of water a day.
- I eat some protein at every meal.
- I snack on raw nuts and sometimes raisins.
- I eat mainly home-cooked meals (more than four times a week).
- I drink vegetable juices like V8 and store-bought vegetable juices with no sugar. Usually these come from the health-food section of the grocery store.
- I occasionally drink a glass of commercially prepared fruit juice.
- I drink only juice made with my juicer.
- I shop carefully and read all labels.
- I never buy any product with an ingredient I can't pronounce.
- I eat fish and chicken regularly.
- I eat red meat only twice per month.
- I buy only organically grown vegetables.

- I buy free range eggs.
- I drink no caffeine products of any kind.
- I never drink pop.
- I feel energetic and only experience a slight fluctuation in my energy levels during the day.
- I eat oils like olive oil, but only in their raw form; I never fry with oil.
- I use butter, but not in excess.
- I know my eating isn't optimal and I am motivated to make some changes.
- I feel content with the way I nourish myself and know that this contributes to my well-being.
- I take some supplements on a daily basis.
- I only buy quality supplements from a health food store or independent market.
- I maintain a gluten-free diet.
- I eat a variety of grains like rye, smelt, and kamut, and I only buy whole grain, high quality bread and eat it sparingly.

Total Score:_____

Choosing to **adhere** to the above activities is also a choice in the direction toward optimal health!

Make a commitment to yourself to eat in a way that will support and not add more stress to your body. From a place of wholeness, it is easier to stay clean, clear and open.

Also very important for keeping your energy clean is getting a proper amount of rest and meeting your need for a good eight to nine hours of sleep a night; this can be an individual thing as some may require less sleep. Your body needs time to restore itself and sleep-deprivation will affect every part of your life.

Emotional Connection to the Meridians

Let's explore energy a bit more. How does it work? Your energy flows along meridian lines in the body, just like electricity flows through a wire. Along these lines are the acupressure points that many kinds of therapists will work on. Acupressure is touch therapy, whereas acupuncture uses needles to work on this energy. Look up "meridian charts" on the internet for images of these meridian lines.

There are fourteen meridians in the human body and each one pairs with another (for example, the liver meridian pairs with the gallbladder meridian); this creates seven pairs. Below you will see a list of these meridian pairs and what emotions are connected to them when they are in balance, and also when they are out of balance. Doing the Transformer 13—Meridian Wash, which you will find in the Transformers section in Chapter 11, is a great way to keep your energy clean. It can take as little as a few minutes and you can feel a shift right away.

Governing/ Central Meridians

These control the brain and spinal cord. When an issue resides in this meridian pair, it is usually systemic and more intense. When this meridian is unbalanced, the emotions associated are feeling vulnerable and having a lack of courage to move forward. **In balance:** associated emotions are an overall sense of strength and a feeling of being centred and balanced.

Liver/ Gallbladder Meridians

This is the seat of primitive emotion. The emotions present when out of balance are anger and resentment. In the gallbladder, the emotion is usually more intense like seething, more of a hidden or suppressed anger. **In balance:** associated emotions are kindness, tolerance, and gentleness to self.

Bladder/ Kidney Meridians

These meridians when unbalanced emote fear, shame, anger (being "pissed off"), and anxiety. This is the meridian pair that usually expresses relationship issues. **In balance:** associated emotions are gentleness to self, resourcefulness, and willingness to move beyond comfort zone.

Large Intestine/ Lung Meridians

When this meridian pair is out of balance, it indicates that a person is holding onto "old stuff", not letting go, being controlling, unexpressed sadness or grief, not breathing in life fully, and a lack of enthusiasm for life. People who express constipation are definitely holding on to "old shit". Sorry! I couldn't resist! When the opposite occurs in the form of diarrhea, this indicates a sense of being overwhelmed and life is moving too fast. They are feeling fearful and want to get away from it all. **In balance:** associated emotions are releasing, letting go of the past, breathing in life, and bringing in joy.

Stomach/ Spleen Meridians

Imbalance here manifests as "I can't stomach this anymore", dread, and worrying. **In balance:** associated emotions are trust and ease.

Triple Warmer/ Circulation Sex Meridians

These are the fight or flight meridians; unbalanced emotions are feeling stressed, nervousness, and depression. **In balance:** associated emotions are feeling safe and happy.

Heart/Small Intestine Meridians

Unbalanced emotions here are heartache, a lack of love, an inability to assimilate and digest life, and not being in flow. **In balance:** associated emotions are self-love and love of others; more in flow with life and the heart is open to receive.

I want to share an amazing example of how meridian work can be manifested. During a training course that I give called "Energy Psychology", I had a student whom we could all feel was experiencing some very heavy energy. During the different learning modules, students take turns being the person whom we work on. Everyone concluded that we needed to work on this student. We determined what the BS was (this is done through muscle testing) and proceeded to do a correction (this is the process to release this limiting pattern). It so happened that this pattern wasn't hers, but her mother's. There was a dramatic stress around her grandmother's birth that this woman had been carrying. Her grandmother's birth was the result of a rape that no one in the family had ever discussed. The student had heard vaguely about it and here it was showing its face in her energy body.

Once we started the correction (we held points on the different meridians and in this case, on all fourteen of them), she manifested the unbalanced emotional response of each particular meridian. It was fascinating to watch. When we were working with the liver meridian, she was growling and expressing anger, while her body moved involuntarily. When we were holding points at the stomach meridian, she was gagging like she was throwing up. In the circulation-sexual meridian, it was as if she was giving birth, and on it went until we were done all the meridians. All these movements were involuntary: she had no control over them. She was exhausted after it was complete; but the trauma had been released. What was amazing was how she had just demonstrated the emotions trapped in each meridian. We all thanked her for her courage to share this with the group.

As I have said, you hold all your experiences in your body, not just in your mind. That is why I feel cleaning our energy is so critical to release stored information and let it go. It can be trapped there in the dark for years, causing all kinds of havoc until we release it to the light and send it packing.

Chapter 5

Go Inside

Your Inner World

How tuned in to your life are you? Take a little time just to notice. What is going on for you as you read this book? Is your inner critic out or are you assimilating this material easily? How is it resonating with you? Just notice. No action is required.

The concept of listening to ourselves needs to be taken to a deeper level. Listening is about being in the state of receiving; about really paying attention. Listen to your own energy—how does it feel? What is really going on for you? Most of us get so caught up in everyday life that we lose sight of our deeper needs. Making choices that will support us is easier when we take the time to really feel whether or not we resonate with our choices. Resonance is like a gut feeling, an intuitive sense of what will be in our highest good. We can only tune in to this awareness if we pay close attention.

There is a quality to your choice and a quality to your energy, and if the two are compatible, then the choice you are making is one that will support you. This taps in to the innate intelligence that we each possess living inside of us; it knows what we need to do for ourselves. There is no need to search extrinsically for what we need: it is right here, with us always. If choices you make are not compatible with your energy, then this will inevitably lead to struggle.

Let me explain a little further. Terry was on leave from work and he was in the process of deciding whether to return to his place of employment or to take an early retirement package. He told me that he had visualized himself sitting at his desk doing his job, and when doing so his entire body had reacted extremely negatively; he felt awful. This is a case where there was no resonance between his choice and his energy: the two were incompatible. Going back to work would only cause Terry angst and lead to more struggles in his life. In the end, he made the courageous choice to start following his heart and to pursue work that would feed his soul, not drain his energy.

Making choices that we resonate with is what really listening to ourselves is all about. This resonance theory can be used with any decision you would like to make and are unsure of. Put yourself in the place of actually doing whatever it is you're thinking of. Let's say you are planning to purchase a new home. Imagine yourself there, walking through the house, lounging in the yard. If there is a comfort there and you feel positive, then this is a choice that you resonate with. However, if on the other hand you feel uncomfortable, unsettled, or unsure, then this may not be a compatible fit. Trust your intuitive senses. They are powerful and can save you enormous grief.

Living this way has brought me a multitude of gifts even with small decisions, such as when to go camping. For example, I was planning a two-day camping trip that I was going to take in about six weeks. I was wondering which days would work the best. So I tuned into myself and looked at the calendar. Then I picked two days that felt good and that I resonated with. It turned out that they were the only two days that week when it didn't rain. The sun shone for my entire trip and then rain poured as soon as I got home. I always marvel at how much easier my life is now, and how many positive things have come into my life since I have begun to really stop, look, and listen.

Resonance

Let's look a little more deeply at resonance and how it can help us gain clarity.

How often have you been in a place where you just can't seem to make a choice? You have many options and just don't know what you really want. Learning how to give the choices to your body and not just your mind is a quick way to find out what is really in your highest good for your best intention, as we saw in the two examples above. Resonance is about putting what you want into the feeling body and seeing how it responds. The options vibrate energetically and when you give them to the body, they will give you information about how this vibration feels.

Another example of this comes from my friend Liz. Liz had wanted to move back to her home country in the United Kingdom, where she would be able to get a really good job in her field. She had been living in Canada with her husband for many years and just couldn't make the decision about whether to move back or not. It was a difficult decision, since her husband was unable to go with her and theirs would become a long-distance relationship. During a resonance exercise which is described below, she put these two choices of staying or going into her feeling body and immediately she could feel the strength behind the choice to go. Within a few months, she made the move and it all flowed with ease. This turned out to be a very positive move for her and she was able to get back into her field of work, be there to support her family in the United Kingdom, and even her relationship went through a time of positive growth.

I had another friend who used this method around making a career choice. She had two job offers and was unsure which one she should take. So she took turns wearing the hat of one job and then the hat of the other. She pretended she was actually doing one job and going through all the actions in her mind and feeling what it would be like, and then she switched to the other job. During that process she figured out which one she wanted to take, based on how this felt. She chose what she resonated with. This is a much more accurate way of gaining information than just trusting your mind to come up with the answer. I personally use this with any choice that I am not sure of and ninety-nine percent of the time I come up with the right choice for myself.

Resonance Exercise

This is how resonance works. You may want to try this cool exercise by yourself or with a friend. This will really tap into your intuition and your body's awareness of what is in your highest good.

If you are doing it on your own, get very quiet and relaxed, and take some deep breaths. Think of a decision you want to make between two choices and vividly imagine them both. Then start thinking of one of the choices and actually experiencing it in your body. Feel yourself doing, being, and living this choice. Then, try the other choice and again be with it and really feel, taste, and smell this choice. Experience both choices as fully as you can. Now reflect what they both felt like. Which one had more resonance to it? When you resonate with a choice it feels comfortable and peaceful. Your body is at ease. Sometimes, it feels like you are "home". This process takes choice away from the logical mind and gives it to your intuitive knowing. This can be a very powerful experience and usually when you are done, you will know which choice is in your highest good.

If you find it hard to do this on your own, ask a friend to guide you through. They can give you some instruction to relax all parts of your body and then take you to the first choice. Then, take a break, be with what that was like and really put that choice into the feeling body. Next, imagine the opposite option. Compare how both feel.

Have fun with it, you may be surprised by what comes up. If both choices feel right, then both choices resonate with your energy and either one will work for you.

Take Time to Self-Reflect

Self-reflection can come in many forms. In the Transformer section, there are many options. Meditation of course is a very powerful way of getting out of your way and really listening, but self-reflection can also mean just sitting quietly out in nature and staring at the trees or ocean, or taking a walk and being with yourself. In our busy, demanding lives, self-reflection is imperative to see the bigger picture and to allow your Source, Creator, to talk to you. It is one of the most precious gifts you can give yourself.

One of my most powerful experiences happened recently. I sat down to meditate and many thoughts were going through my mind. I just watched them, and then something happened. A stillness came over me. It was like a hum; I could feel my energy and I knew intuitively that this was my eternal self. It was as if I was just observing my energy, my own life force. I knew I was eternal, infinite, and that I was tapping into my spirit. It made the mind, with all its shenanigans, seem so meaningless and such an illusion. This energy was expansive, but the quality of it seemed like a clean slate. If this is who I really am, then, Wow! I can be and do anything! With a clean slate, I can imprint anything on it.

I knew this was an enlightened experience and it totally changed my life. This is an excerpt from my journal about this experience:

> "In that nothingness, that clean slate with no agenda, anything is possible through the formless. There are no limitations, only miracles, because in the eternal, nothing-state there are no beliefs; beliefs are human ego forms. There are only creation and expansion. These are states of God/Creator. So when the empty space projects onto the formless, anything can happen, because God/Formless Creation reacts to the observer, and when the observer is not attached to ego stuff, it too is limitless."

This experience took some digesting, challenging my old beliefs about what God/Creator really is. This seemed much more in line with Buddhist philosophy, which I very much resonate with. I sought out my dear minister friend to discuss this with. What she said really made sense. I asked her about this clean slate, this eternal self that I experienced as God/Creator and how it seemed opposite from how religions always talk about a loving or a punitive God. In many religions, God is portrayed as a being, separate from us, but as the creative force in the Universe, the absolute law that what you ask for you shall receive. She said, "God is not personal; God is neutral, and loving in the way that it is giving: it will give you what you believe and what you are putting forth. So if you wake up one day and say, 'I am having a bad day,' this giving energy will give you back what you put out. So, be careful what you ask for. This loving/giving energy says yes to whatever belief we are putting into the world, whether consciously or unconsciously." Her explanation made me even more determined to act intentionally in my life and imprint a positive loving blueprint on my clean slate.

Grass Hut Syndrome

There are times in our lives when we need to take the time to just go inside. Sometimes this need is more than just reflecting and feels more like an inner retreat. I envision a grass hut somewhere in the middle of nowhere—where I am all by myself. I call this the "grass hut syndrome", where I just don't want to be with anyone and just need to be alone, to be with my God essence, let go of the outside world, and just be. It's not always easy in our busy lives, but it is important to take this time, even if it's just a day to stay in bed and do nothing but allow yourself some "me time" and to see who is home. Is it your happy self or are you feeling depleted? Then take some time to see what it is you need to do for yourself. The more you heed these messages, the less often you have to retreat into your grass hut. It's when we get to a place of utter depletion that the outside world just seems too much. I have found that when I get to this place, it is usually an indicator that growth is imminent, and the growth is about letting go and moving to an even deeper understanding of who I am. Sometimes, these times can feel like "dark nights of the soul", when I feel like, "Okay, I am done with this human experience and I just want to go and play with the angels." Being a spirit having a human experience isn't always easy. The quicker you can get to the letting go, the easier it is to transcend this space and feel joy again in the human experience.

Chapter 6

Open the Pathway

How to Clear Your Way Forward through Acceptance

Hanging onto the past and not accepting "what is" is a sure fire way to keep a person stuck. Sometimes the journey to create the life we want doesn't move fast enough for some folks. I saw this so often with my clients. They would get so frustrated about their lack of moving forward that they would get themselves stuck. Acceptance doesn't mean you don't want things to change; it just means you honour where you are on the journey at the time. From this place of acceptance, it is much easier to move ahead.

We are all going to have challenging circumstances in our lives, whether it be a marriage ending, a job we have felt secure in that is coming to a close, personal illness, illness with family members, needy aging parents, difficulties with our children, loss of a loved one, a world crisis; you name it. Life can change dramatically and offer up a wide variety of circumstances to challenge us. The key to moving with these changes and dealing with whatever challenge that presents itself is to *accept them*, exactly the way things are.

All suffering comes from wanting things to be different than they are. As Buddha said, "suffering is optional". This doesn't mean you have to like the situation, or that you can't change it, but wasting energy wishing it hadn't happened or playing the "what if" game just takes you away from actually dealing with the challenge and finding solutions.

A long while back, I went through a serious depression. I felt like I was fighting it tooth and nail. I expended so much energy thinking, "Why me? Why is this happening? I want this to go away." The inner conflict was draining me more than the actual depression and I had no resources to find the solution, because I was too busy fighting it. I finally came to a place of acceptance. Yes, I was depressed, and this truth was part of my experience. I could then take more of an observer role and it was easier to focus on the solution.

So, whatever life has to offer, once you accept it as part of your experience and just be with it, then you can find creative ways to deal with those challenges. Instead of fighting life, look at what the circumstance has to offer. I have found that all the challenges I have experienced have led to a much richer, fuller life, and have actually helped me. Again, it's a matter of perception.

Challenges are going to present themselves, but how you handle them will determine whether they are gifts or curses.

Native Canadian lore says that an eagle knows when a storm is approaching long before it breaks. The eagle will fly to some high spot and wait for the winds to come. When the storm hits, the eagle sets its wings so that it is picked up and lifted above the storm. While the storm rages below, the eagle is soaring above it. The eagle does not escape the storm. It simply uses the storm to lift it higher. It rises on the winds that bring the storm. When the storms of life come upon us—and all of us will experience them—we can rise above them by setting our minds and our belief toward the positive, spreading our wings and having the courage to leap, trusting that we will not fall, but be carried higher on the strength of something greater and more powerful than ourselves. The storms do not have to overcome us. We can allow positive power within us to lift us above them. We too can soar above the storm.

This acceptance of circumstances and experiences is about the externals in our lives. However, it also pertains to acceptance of our inner difficulties, our inner challenges, what I call my "inner alligators". Whatever your inner alligators are—whether they are fears, old hurts, anger, grief, or negative self-talk—you need to acknowledge their presence and accept that they are part of your psyche before you can say goodbye to them. We can't release what we don't know exists. Dare to dance and face the dark parts of yourself. This can be difficult, but essential in freeing yourself from their hold. Learn to pirouette with your inner alligators and learn what makes them tick. Understanding yourself and the shadows of your personality will empower you. Being honest and allowing yourself to be with your inner discomforts helps to honour all parts of yourself, and can create an inner power that cannot be achieved by avoiding them. This way you aren't going to be surprised when something comes up from behind and hits you in the back of your head when you aren't looking. You can face it, dance with it, and make peace with it, perhaps even learn to love it. This places you in a space of inner power.

Alberto Villoldo says it so well in his book, *The Four Insights*: "When you own the parts of yourself that make you feel uncomfortable, you no longer hold anyone else responsible for your pain or happiness. Then you shine with your own light, like the sun, which is the only thing that casts no shadow."

Accepting ourselves with all our dented pieces, and valuing and loving all parts of ourselves, make it easier to move past our flaws. When we truly value who we are in this human experience, then this spiritual journey we are all on becomes much easier.

Clinical psychologist Tara Brach sums it up in her book, *Radical Acceptance* (Bantam, 2003): "As you go through your day, pause occasionally to ask yourself, this moment do I accept myself just as I am?"

Acceptance is the precursor to letting go and flowing with life rather than trying to control it with every fibre of your being. Controlling life is exhausting. Imagine yourself floating on your back in the water. The more you let go, the easier it is to just lie flat and relax. As soon as you tighten your muscles, you feel yourself sinking. When you let go and relax, the water will totally support you. This is the way it is with life. The more we fuss and muss and try to insist that things go our way, the more tension we create. Loosening the grip and allowing life to flow is much easier. These seeds of peace are inside of all of us: they just need to be nurtured and watered and they will grow and blossom.

Flowing with Life

One of the major lessons I have had in my own life is to learn to flow with life and not let my mind, with all its old conditioning, rule my actions. Most of the time, the mind is based on the old programming that we carry and not on what our hearts and spirit desire. So I have learned to get out of my own way and let my life flow.

I have pushed many rocks up many hills in the past. Trying to make something happen with pure will and not tuning within are very exhausting and usually don't work. I am grateful that I no longer need to do these things.

Dr. Eric Pearl, the founder of Reconnective Healing®, says, "The less you try to direct, the more room you give the Universe to do so—and the greater the results. It's not that the Universe can't work around you; it's just that there's a certain level of grace and ease that occurs when you get yourself out of the way."

We are all so busy trying to make things happen that we strangle the energy around the very thing that we want to create. It's almost like we put an energy vice on what we want and it can't move. When we create space around what we want to manifest by having an open heart and not "wanting" but rather keeping a joyous focus, then we can start to draw to us that which we desire.

Lama Gendun Rinpoche offers "Key Instructions" for living that say this so clearly:

> Happiness cannot be found through great effort and will power,
> But is already there in relaxation and letting-go
> Don't strain yourself; there is nothing to do . . .
> Only our search for happiness prevents us from seeing it . . .
> Don't believe in the reality of good and bad experiences
> They are like rainbows.
> Wanting to grasp the ungraspable, you exhaust yourself in vain.
> As soon as you relax this grasping, space is there
> —open, inviting, and comfortable.
> So make use of it. All is yours already
> Don't search any further . . .
> Nothing to do
> Nothing to force,
> Nothing to want,
> —and everything happens by itself.

This attitude of relaxing into life is so liberating. Ideas then can come easily and effortlessly without stress and strain.

Getting Out of My Own Way

A while back, I had a profound insight that it was time to make major changes in my life. I needed to leave my self-employment, sell my house, and move across Canada to the West Coast. I felt energetically that where I was living was pulling me down and that it was time to move. Every location has its own energy and if we are not a match to this energy, it can drain our life force. I'd had a desire for a long time to move to British Columbia.

At first, the prospect of starting a whole new life was frightening and my mind went into all the "what if's" and "how to's", and into all the things that could go wrong if I made this huge move. After some angst and using some of the Transformers I share in this book, I was able to get out of my own way and just go with the flow. Once I did this, an amazing sense of peace overcame me and I felt in flow and in tune with this decision. I had no job to go to, no specific place to live, but I kept moving forward with the knowledge that it would all unfold exactly the way it was meant to.

I had been self-employed as a teacher and wellness consultant for over ten years and I was ready to leave it behind. I had no desire to go back to my previous career in social work. As I made space in my thoughts for new things to come, an old dream from when I was a teenager re-emerged. I had always wanted to be a flight attendant, and pull a rolly bag around the airport! It looked like a job that offered such freedom and I longed to travel. Initially, life had different plans and I had never realized that dream, though it kept calling to me. Of course, my mind with all its old conditioning started throwing up emotional blockades: "You are too old to become a flight attendant now," etc.... Fortunately, I didn't listen and just took one simple step toward this dream: I applied to a company that had a progressive ideology and seemed to be a great place to work.

I didn't sit around waiting though; I moved forward with my intentions. I sold my house, sold all my belongings, and on the day I was having a house content sale, the airline called and offered me an interview. I had prepared the stage by acting on my intention and the Universe responded.

So at fifty-six years of age, I became a flight attendant with WestJet, the company I had applied to, and I moved across Canada and opened doors

I never thought would open. When we are in tune with our heart's desire, mountains can move easily and life unfolds with grace. I am so grateful I left the rock-pushing behind and now, without all the grasping, life just flows with so much more ease.

Another important issue around flow is timing. Our ego may have its own idea of when something "should" happen, but it may not be aligned with the right time for something to happen. When there is ease, then the time is right. If you are struggling with a choice, an emotion or a thought, then it isn't the right time. Change your focus to something that is in flow and let it all unfold. Forcing something into being is just exhausting and could take you down a road that isn't in your highest good. When the time is right, things just show up, and you would be amazed at the speed with which your highest good can happen when all is aligned and your heart is open.

A friend shared a really neat story about being in flow. She was getting dressed for work, and thought, "I wish I had a pair of red earrings to go with this outfit." At different points during the day, she kept thinking about having red earrings. Later that day, her daughter returned from a vacation and presented her with a gift. Before her daughter even handed the small box to her, my friend quizzed her daughter, "Are those red earrings?" Her daughter's jaw dropped and she said, "How did you know?" Inside were the red earrings she had wished for! This is a great example of someone being in flow and tuning into her daughter's energy.

Doing Versus Flowing: Yang and Yin

We live in a male-dominated society where "doing" is revered over "being". I call this the "Masculine D energies": all the doing, dealing, demanding. This is the *yang* male energy that is more about the outer world that dominates most societies. I associate this with major rock-pushing up hills, which can be exhausting! We all do it: males and females alike. We admire people who have "made it" on their own, and who "pull themselves up by their bootstraps", and who "just do it". Alberto Villoldo says, "It's difficult for us in the West to trust we can achieve peace and happiness if we're not doing something active to bring it about. But embodying peace and happiness does bring it about. Our egos don't want us to believe that we can have infinite power by immersing ourselves in the wisdom of the Universe, but it's true" (*The Four Insights*). This comes from being, rather than doing. It is so counter-intuitive to what many of us have been taught that it is difficult to fully comprehend.

This yang energy, when exploited and out of control as it is in our world, depletes the soul and leaves a gaping wound in everyone and everything. When this energy is dominant in our lives, we aren't open to receiving the love and nurturance that we all so desperately need and deserve.

Then there is the feminine, *yin*, "Feminine R energy," with its **receiving, reflecting, and remembering**. This is more about our inner world. This energy has remained in the background for centuries but is coming forward during this era. Our world so desperately needs this softer, nurturing yin energy to heal our planet. We need the dominant, male energy, which is focused on separateness, to get out of the way in order to open up space for the nurturing, soft energy that is about connectedness. In my opinion this will bring our societies to a place where we can all work together to heal the wound of separateness we all carry. As the yin-yang symbol graphically depicts, both are equal, balancing each other. Up until now, the yang energy is prevalent on the planet, and is wreaking havoc on balance in all forms.

My own personal journey to this point had been about a lack of nurturance and mothering as a young child. I lived with a mother who had mental health issues and a limited ability to nurture since she had not experienced nurturing in her own life either. With this lack of female nurturing energy, I had created a very male yang energy for myself.

One day while attending a conference, I met the earth angel and sacred singer, Denise Hagan; she is someone who epitomizes this female, pink, nurturing energy. She had just come over from Ireland. She was invited to come to the stage during the conference and sing, and she sang a beautiful song with such a nurturing, loving energy in every word that I just started to weep. I wept as I remembered this loving energy that is available to all of us. I wept for missing it for so long. I wept for all of us who have had to struggle through male "masculine D energy", feeling that it is the way we are supposed to be.

This earth angel brought such a gift into my life of helping me develop the soft yin energy and feeling that I deserve to be loved, probably for the first time. It was a very pivotal point in my life and opened my heart wider than it had been opened before. It brought a more balanced approach to my life.

Our society has leaned toward the male, yang, doing energy and now we need to find more balance where both yang and yin are used in harmony with each other. Both energies are needed. If we open our hearts to receive but do not move our feet, we may be waiting for a long time for our intentions to come to fruition. If we are dominant in the doing energy we may end up spinning our wheels and miss opportunities that can come from just waiting and letting go. Dr. Eric Pearl says, "The freedom of being will extricate you from the oppression of doing."

How do you know when you are in yang energy? Usually in this state, the mind is dominating. You could be making lists, trying to control, and being preoccupied with the outcome. You are using your mind in isolation from the heart to guide you. Yin energy is softer, feeling energy; you tend to be more relaxed about how you are thinking. There isn't rigidity to your thinking and your heart is leading the way. Working with the mind and heart in unison, using both the yin and the yang energy, is a balanced way to live our lives; it's how we can open doors to miracles.

Since we tend to live in a more dominant, yang way of operating in the world, cultivating our yin, softer energy is something many of us need to practise. So when you find yourself in a doing, yang mode, pull back; just watch and notice. Is your mind in a frantic mode trying to get results? Are you pushing your energy? Sometimes it is powerful to stay in the not knowing, being open to just let things happen when the time is right. I have had to be in this empty, open, nothing place very often and for me, being a doer, this has at times been challenging. I have learned that being in the not-knowing place, the abyss, can be a very freeing place and life can then just unfold with such grace it can take your breath away. This is the God zone and can leave you in absolute awe of how life can be when we get out of our way!

Is Your Past Following You?

Cultivating inner peace has been an intention that I have adhered to, and it has brought with it enormous gifts. Before my mother died, we had some warning that she was failing; I had time to be with her and reflect on our experience together. As I have said earlier, our relationship had not been an easy one and at times, it was very painful. I was the vessel into which she poured her disappointments in life, and she had many of them. As a friend once put it, "Not all mothers bake cookies."

However, for five years before she died, I enjoyed a healed relationship with my mother, and our time together was warm and peaceful. I was extremely grateful for this warmth when she died. I felt peaceful about her death and, though I would miss her, I knew that it was time for her to go. Her quality of life had diminished and she was ready. I also felt ready to let her go because I had nothing left to say, nothing left to do. It had all been said and done, and we were at peace with each other. That made her death a very different experience. I had learned resilience and compassion from this lady and I chose to focus on that part of my experience with her, not on all the challenges that we had faced. They had been precious lessons that helped me reach inside and find out who I really was.

A dear friend officiated our memorial gathering and he told marvellous stories about my mother, some very humorous that made us all laugh, even though we were in pain for her loss. I had not heard some of the stories before, and I marvelled at how it really is all about our perceptions. My friend had seen a very different side of my mother, which I hadn't focused on, and his sharing this wonderful side of her with us made me see her in this light as well. I was grateful that I could say goodbye with warm memories.

Cultivating peace and not allowing your past to dictate your future is the road to ease. It will have enormous benefits on your physical, mental, and emotional well-being.

Are there any issues from your past that are still in your driver's seat? Are they dictating choices you make? Are you making choices from your clean slate or based on past decisions and experiences? Are you holding onto any past resentment? If so, how does that feel? Is there anything else you are holding onto from your past? Are you resisting letting it go? If so, is that working for you? How much lighter would you feel if you let all that go? Is there anyone you need to forgive? Is there any action that you need to take to release these limitations?

Relationships and Their Role in Our Getting Out of Our Own Way

Relationships can be huge teachers: they have an enormous impact on our growth, but they can also keep us stuck if we can't see their benefits. We may hold resentments about them and see them as struggles instead of the gifts that they really are. Blaming others for our unhappiness is just a way of discharging our own pain and discomfort. When we blame and dump on others, we feel better about ourselves. But this is temporary. The way to freedom is taking responsibility for our own challenges and not blaming them on others. Many stay stuck in this drama all their lives. I remember my Mom being so mad at my Dad for taking her away from her homeland and bringing her to Canada; fifty years later, she was still bringing this issue up to him and holding onto the anger. I suggested that perhaps she should let this go; but to no avail.

I think if we understand the amazing roles relationships have in our lives, we could deal with them more easily, see their purpose, and not get too attached to the drama. This would be so helpful in getting out of our way; just seeing our relationships in a different light, as tools and guides to help us grow. Understanding their role in our evolution will transform some of your most challenging relationships into insights into yourself.

My dear friend Lori and I had an amazing conversation about this during one of our many camping adventures. We talked about "soul categories" as a way to understand the types of relationships we have encountered in our lives, relationships that are there to help us grow. I came up with three categories that seemed to be prevalent in my life.

The first category is the Soul Teachers. These are people who had come into my life (my Mom is one of them) to help me grow by pushing every button and really making me see where I need healing. As challenging as these relationships are, their role in my evolution has been critical and without them I would not be where I am today. So I thank them and recognize the valuable role they have played.

If you don't learn the lesson and just abandon the relationship, another person will come along to resume the drama. Until we understand the role that people play in our lives, we will continue to perpetuate the drama. Once we see the gift, we can take it graciously, get out of our way, and heal what it is they are making us see. And interestingly, once we heal that relationship, those dramas and issues that the relationship represents disappear from our lives. The lesson has been learned.

The second category comprises my Soul Support group. These are friends I have known for many years, one since I was a teenager. I see them as wonderful support companions on this journey. One in particular was an earth angel when I was a teenager; her help and support throughout my life has been immense. We often went for years without seeing each other but then would reconnect and the connection was always easy and fun. We may not share a deep spiritual connection with these people, but their support is invaluable.

The third category is my Spirit Soul group. These are folks that I have a deep spiritual connection with. These are friends who support my journey by seeing all that I am and all that I can become. They are like my cheerleaders and are so gracious in their loving support. They encourage me, and the connection is always easy and heartfelt. These are the relationships in which I feel free to explore spiritual matters and to ask and share anything. Dark places can be shared, and acceptance and support is always received.

I am grateful that the more I have grown and evolved, the less I encounter the Soul Teachers; instead I gravitate to my Soul Support and Spirit Soul groups. Boy, this sure makes life easier. Until we see the gifts our Soul Teachers bring us and really honestly look at ourselves with a willingness to heal what they bring up, we will continue to attract these folks into our lives until we get it.

Chapter 7

Being at One

Are Your Heart and Mind at One with Each Other?

The HeartMath Institute in California was founded in 1991 by Doc Childre. Its mission is *"to facilitate a fundamental shift in health, well-being and consciousness" (www.heartmath.com). It* has done some fascinating studies on the heart. Their studies say that the heart has its own intrinsic nervous system and processes information independently of the brain and the nervous system, even though the brain, providing yang dominant energy, can quite often trump the heart. The heart was reclassified as an endocrine gland (glands that controls the hormones) in 1983; it secretes its own hormones that affect other organs in the body and the brain. The heart profoundly affects our perception and intelligence.

The heart is also the centre of our connection to our higher intelligence. Staying heart-centred has a profound effect on all aspects of life: physical, emotional, and spiritual. It is a common experience that when a lifelong spouse dies the other spouse is "heartbroken". Typically it is not long after that when they also leave this life. As the HeartMath study concludes, the heart has an enormous effect on the whole body.

Keeping your energy clean and your heart open are imperative for getting out of your own way. Joseph Campbell states, "The goal of life is to make your heartbeat match the beat of the cosmos to match your nature with Nature." In their book *Your Soul's Compass*, Joan Borysenko and Gordon Dveirin say, "Our awakened heart is the receiver that picks up the signal for the Divine Heart. We in turn transmit that love. Synchronicities appear as we come into coherence with a larger field, and guidance opens the way before us: the scientist receives inspiration, an idea for a book just shows up. Following the thread of love, excitement, passion, gratitude, we find the treasure."

A simple example of synchronicity in my own life happened just recently. I was having an adventure with my grandson, who is eight. We call our adventures "Cole/Mummu adventures" (*Mummu* means "grandmother" in Finnish) and we both love these times together to explore and just hang out. My heart is always extra open when we are together and it shows in what turns up. On this particular adventure, we were heading into the city and we both desperately needed to use the washroom. It was market day when parking is usually at a premium. A metered parking area near the public washroom had only about a dozen spots, but it was the most convenient. So Cole and I summoned the "parking angels" and asked for a spot; sure enough as we pulled into this lot, one car was just pulling out and we got the only spot available. We both laughed with joy. Our timing was impeccable because our hearts were open, and magic always happens from this place of openness.

An open heart receives many gifts; a closed one pushes them away. How open is your heart? If you allowed yourself to be totally open, what would you really desire? Go inside and do a "heart checkup" and see how it is feeling. Are there any hurts still residing in there that you need to let go of?

Operating through the heart is the way to create miracles, but what really creates a powerful force is when the heart and mind are aligned and working together. The West tends to consider feeling and thinking as opposites if not antagonists. However, in eastern medicine, heart and mind are closely associated and their unity is vital for health.

A split between mind and heart, in which they are working at odds with each other, creates blocks to health and spiritual wholeness. Happily, when we become aware of this split we can focus on the union of heart (source) and the mind (ego) and make our journey a much easier one. Carl Jung, a pioneer in the field of understanding our inner selves, saw how imperative it was for societies to start leading with their hearts and not with the logical mind, which just presents conditioned responses rather than authentic experiences. Jung felt himself led to a profound insight into the imbalance in western civilizations. Even Jung, a pioneer of psychoanalysis, was taken by surprise when he came to this conclusion.

Although many people will readily admit that they use their heads to chart all aspects of their daily lives and suffer a lot of anxiety as they do, few seem to recognize that their internal angst is in fact generated by the loss of connection to their heart centre. Our spiritual and energetic centres are in our heart and when we stay heart-focused, we are closer to who we really are beyond the limitations of the mind.

Here is a brief look at the oppositions that can go on between heart and mind:

Heart builds on faith that success is possible.
Brain needs proof that failure can be avoided.

Heart reaches forward.
Brain holds onto the past.

Heart embraces what's possible.
Brain clings to what is "realistic".

Heart celebrates victory.
Brain judges failure.

Heart plays.
Brain works.

Heart wishes for the best.
Brain assumes the worst.

Heart tends to speak in terms of "us".
Brain uses "me" and "you".

Heart pilots, guided by the stars.
Brain steers, looking in the rearview mirror.

Which voice is playing in your head?

The heart is a powerful force and carries the imprint of the soul. It is the pathway to our life force and when the mind is aligned with its creative powers, miracles are a given. The heart and mind in unison can be an even more powerful force to be reckoned with.

Let's talk a little more about what the heart actually does other than the physical aspect of actually keeping us live. The heart is a huge magnetic force that will draw to us what feels good. With feeling energy, this force becomes a magnet that pulls in the same energy you are putting out. Have you ever met someone who is so positive and joyful that you just seem drawn to them? That is the magnetic force pulling you in. The heart is also the "mother energy": the being, nurturing yin energy. The mind is more the yang, father, doing energy. When you have the power of the mind and the power of the heart working for you, you are limitless. Your mind can come up with creative ideas that are fed with inspiration from your life force and channelled through the heart. Then, it's full speed ahead with your desires!

You may be thinking, "Okay, this sounds really good, but how do I get there?" It takes focused energy to keep your mind from running amok. There are many Transformers in Chapter 11 to help you stay focused and to open the heart, like Transformer 11—Three Heart Energy Exercises. The most important step you can take is to set the intention that you want to lead with your heart and let your heart service your mind, not the other way around, which is how most of us operate.

One weekend, a friend and I went to visit another friend to spend a few days together. My two friends did not know each other very well, but there seemed to be a lovely synergy between the three of us. On the first day of our visit we had no agenda and just decided to have a free-flowing day. We went to the local market and for long walks in the park. There just seemed to be such a flow between us but also within each of us. Our hearts were open and our minds were aligned with our hearts. Synchronistic events were a constant.

At one point as we were walking through the park, Lori was thinking to herself about how she had left her deodorant—of all things—at home. As we continued walking, we came upon some men dressed in "Degree" costumes who were promoting a product—you guessed it: Degree de-odorant! One handed a sample to Lori, not to anyone else, but to Lori who was the one who had been thinking about having no deodorant! We just laughed. What were the odds?

Then, when we were in the market, I was drawn to a beautiful painting of trees. There was a mystical feel to it. I went to purchase it, but the vendor did not take credit cards and none of us had enough cash. I walked away thinking it just wasn't meant to be. Then as we were leaving I just couldn't go. We went back to see the vendor, to ask him if he would be there next week when my friend could pick it up for me. There was something about the man that seemed familiar and it turned out he was of Finnish descent like me and was born in the same area my Dad was, which is now part of Russia. We immediately began to speak in our language and it was such a wonderful connection. He then said, "Just take the painting and send me a cheque." I was so moved by his trust and it was such a magical experience.

The whole day was like that. One synchronistic event after another. The three of us were so in awe of this wonderful, magical day and knew we were definitely in flow with powerful forces in the Universe, but what was also taking place is that each one of us was operating with our hearts and minds in unison so that we were in tune to this magical flow. I find that the more I allow my heart and mind to be at one, the more magic seems to show up.

Another instance that demonstrates the power of the mind and heart working together happened during a camping trip. My friend was supposed to come with me, but her dad was gravely ill and she was unable to make the trip. I just felt there must be a reason and headed off on the camping trip by myself.

On my last day, I was heading home feeling very peaceful and not really thinking about anything. I was just enjoying the drive and feeling in flow. All of a sudden, thoughts about a course that I had no intention of teaching started to flow through me. The ideas were fast and constant. I finally had to pull over and get out some paper and start writing all the ideas down. I had been an energy worker for about fifteen years and had developed my own system, a combination of other modalities I had learned, but I had never thought of amalgamating them into one system. Here it was; it just seemed to download into my consciousness. The whole course with all the modules came to me, along with the knowledge that I was supposed to teach it.

This has now turned into my energy psychology training course based on the energetic kinesiology I studied. I was so excited about this new inspiration and it was quite a turning point. I had been a teacher before at a local college and had taught a variety of courses, but once I moved to British Columbia, I had not thought of going down this path again and certainly had not thought of creating a whole new course. Here it was! This was my heart and mind working in unison and tapping into Divine intelligence to produce these amazing ideas. No effort was required; it just poured out easily and with immense joy. If my friend had joined me, this never would have occurred. The synchronicities of life still amaze me.

Separation Versus Working in Unison

Our society is very focused on the illusion of separateness. Dr. Eric Pearl says: "Healing is the restoration of the person to spiritual wholeness. In essence, healing is this: the release of a block or interference that has kept us separate from the perfection of the Universe".

I think our journey here is to connect to the oneness that is our true nature. We all breathe the same air and our energies are all interconnected. When we can join with our fellow humans, find collective solutions to life's challenges, and work in harmony, what a better world this will be. When we can join with the force that created us and use our force for the betterment of all, enormous healing can result. Creation knows that our world needs a huge dose of healing.

Gregg Braden expands on this idea in *Spontaneous Healing of Belief:* "Perhaps the great hurt that underlies all others is the pain of separation from the greater existence. If this is true, then maybe we miss our larger soul family so much that we try to fill the void by creating a sense of unity through smaller falsities here on earth. It's no wonder that their loss can be so devastating to us. It throws us right back into the pain of the original hurt".

An us-versus-them mentality seems to be prevalent. Most corporations seem to operate this way. Working in isolation from one another tends to be the norm. I think when we operate this way, we are not tuned in, tapped in, and turned on to each other; we work in our own void.

I feel very grateful that I work as a flight attendant for an airline or-ganization that is very different from that norm. That is why I chose to work there. We work in an equity-based system (which means there is no seniority) and the employees are also owners. This allows everyone to have a say in how they think we should operate. Twice a year, we are rewarded for our good work and we get a share of the profits. This is always the time when the company celebrates what we have accomplished together! It's not a perfect system, but it is more inclusive than most, and people feel like they have a say in how the organization is run and a say in what matters to them. One of the concepts that we work under is called the "one crew concept" where you work together as a crew. So when we have to clean our plane before the next guests arrive, the pilots come out of the flight deck and clean garbage out of the seat pockets just like the rest of us. When we finish a flight and leave to either go home or to the hotel, we wait for each other and go off as a group. We each have a different expertise, of course, but we value each person's role and work together to get the job done. It is a wonderful culture to work in and very different from anything else I have experienced. In this day of economic challenges, this company is thriving, as is evidenced by our profit-sharing cheques.

I saw a beautiful example of union and humanity at its best one day on the plane. I was lead, which means I was working at the front, greeting guests onto the plane. We were boarding our special guests and the Customer Service Agent brought down a very elderly lady in a wheel chair clutching her cane and purse. She wore a scarf on her head and was dressed in European clothing; she looked rather weary. The agent announced, "This lady is Ukrainian and speaks NO English." I smiled at her and tried to reassure her that we would take good care of her even though I knew she didn't understand a word I said. She lovingly kissed the hand of the Customer Service Agent and they nodded good bye. I was about to get her into her seat in the front row when her seat mate stood up immediately and started helping me get her seated and buckled in. She was a business woman in her forties who travelled frequently. We got our guest settled, when along came her other seat mate. He was about twenty years old. I immediately explained that our guest didn't speak any English. He smiled at her and said, "Too bad I only speak Siberian."

As the flight progressed, the two seat mates were very kind and helpful whenever our guest needed anything. But that didn't prepare me for what I witnessed next. It still brings tears to my eyes even as I write this.

We had secured the airplane and were on our descent. I had tried to explain that we were descending to our guest and hoped she understood my sign language. I was settled in my jump seat, the one that flight attendants sit in for takeoff and landing, and I looked over in amazement as the business woman had both her hands lovingly clutching the elderly lady's hand, and then I noticed her other hand was also being lovingly held by the young man next to her. Three different generations and no language to connect them but love and caring!

The three of them sat there lost in their thoughts just holding hands for about fifteen minutes. My heart filled as I witnessed this loving gesture and I could feel the tears run down my cheek. When we were waiting to de-plane, I gave the young gentleman a hug and said, "Your Mom would be very proud of you." As we de-planed and I got our guest settled in her wheelchair, she reached out and kissed my cheek and we said our goodbyes. When we were done and I was on my way home, I checked in the baggage area just to make sure our guest was being met by family. Both her seat mates came up to me and were also concerned that she be met. Her eyes lit up when her young grandson met her, and all was well.

I thought of this incident for days and every time I did, my heart filled with such emotion. What would our world be like if we all just held hands and took care of each other?

I had witnessed the very best in humanity and knew even though these folks would never see each other again they shared love and kindness and that I, the witness, would never forget.

Chapter 8

Creating What You Really Desire

Navigating the Blocks

I think that much of the information about the "law of attraction" doesn't really explain the true story of how we create what we really desire. Attraction is an idea that comes from a linear mindset that we are separate from what we desire. When we already see it as part of us and we keep focused on it, then we are unified with this thing, experience, or person that we want to manifest and it will just show up.

I would like to de-mystify how we create what we desire. As we have spoken about earlier, there are conscious and unconscious beliefs that can get in our way. If you have a desire, for example, to have a certain amount of income, or own a home, or whatever requires financial abundance, yet you still hold poverty consciousness (which may even be back in your ancestry), then you will continue meeting blocks, and struggle. Any time you have a conflicting belief, this equals struggle. On one hand, you believe you can have whatever it is, yet your unconscious belief says the opposite. Therefore you are not in flow and will meet with obstacles.

Another key factor I have found in my own life is "wanting". When there is an energy of "wanting" something, or feeling like you just have to have it, whatever it is, that creates an instant block; or you may succeed in creating what you want, but not in a way that is truly for your highest good or what you had precisely intended. You can feel this "wanting" in your gut. There is neediness to this energy and it is an instant squelcher of our dreams.

Another factor which is closely related is having expectations. How many times have you been disappointed because you created expectations of yourself or others? How did you feel when your expectations were not met? Intentions are needed in order to let the Universe know what you desire; but expectations are of the ego. This neediness always comes from fear. When your intentions are pure and have no neediness attached to them, then you are plugged into the source, and manifestation is easy. Attach joy to your dreams and watch them flourish; attach neediness or wanting and watch them fade.

Another way we block our dreams is by pushing energy out. As we have said, we are all energy beings—everything is just energy and information. If there is a desire, let's say it's a workshop you want to teach and you feel you need to get a certain number of participants, you then take action from a place of need: this creates a pushing out of your energy. Your action is not inspiration but action, based on a need to make it happen and to get people to come. If your energy is "out there", it is not "in here" and you are depleting your life force. We are not meant to force our energy, but to be open to receiving it. That is a very different energy. Receiving is easy; pushing energy is hard. This pushing-rocks-up-hills energy gets inferior results and is exhausting. When we are in a receiving mode, we have more resources to work with. We are meant to flow with life and let it unfold. Be a receiver not a pusher, and you will find life so much easier. Where in your life are you pushing energy and forcing your will? How is that working for you?

Another block people create is timelines. At times, I still need to get out of my own way and allow things to unfold without having to set a timeline, such as saying "By November 30, 20XX, I will have …" The formless doesn't do timelines! My background as a behavioural therapist was riddled with timelines.

Sometimes, if you have a gut feeling and know that whatever you desire will occur, then a timeline can work. If this timeline is coming from your mind—it's just an ego function. Let go of "when" and instead hold it close to your heart in knowing it will happen, and get out of the way! When the feeling for what you want comes truly from the heart with an open and expansive energy, and you are in flow and aligned, it will easily come to you. I have found that when I get out of my way and allow things to unfold when they are meant to unfold without expectations, things just happen easily.

A huge block for many is fear. Fright is instinctual, but fear is a learned response. If it is learned, then it can be unlearned.

In my past, fear seemed to consume me. As a child, I was afraid of everything, from candles to heights, from water to bridges. As a young adult in my first apartment, I slept with my shoes and coat by my bed in case there was a fire. I was constantly on alert. It was exhausting. As I grew into adulthood, some of those fears faded, but more subtle ones replaced them: being afraid to make a phone call for fear of rejection; fear of failing; fear of pursuing my dreams; and even fear of losing everything and being a bag lady—not sure where that came from, but it was there. I saw how these fears were ruling my life and limiting me. So about ten years ago, I decided it was time to tackle these demons. I thought of my biggest possible fear and jumping out of an airplane was pretty high up there. So, I decided to tackle this fear, and skydive. I don't necessarily recommend this as form of therapy, but it did work for me.

When the day came, I was absolutely terrified and was sitting in the airplane clutching onto the doorframe with white knuckles when my instructor (who was jumping with me in tandem) said quietly into my ear, "You have to let go." As I did, out I went. It was an exhilarating experience! Once I opened my eyes and the parachute opened, I left a lot of my fears behind in that sky. That gave me courage to do many of the things that I had once been so afraid of. I kept a picture of that experience on my desk to help me remember: "If I can do that, I can do anything".

Though I made an enormous leap forward, I still found fear a regular companion, until a few years later I had just had enough and did an energy correction on my own, one by one, by holding points on all the fourteen meridians I discussed earlierMany of the negative patterns and BS are carried in our cells and tissues, as evidenced by Dr. Candace Pert's research. That is why I feel releasing this energy can have such profound effects. My energy correction had dramatic results. I could feel the release as my body shook and twitched. I finally was able to leave my fears behind and now, I feel I lead a fairly fearless life, which has opened up so many doors for me.

Own your fears. If you push them aside, they can come up when you least expect them and smack you in the back of the head—not a pleasant experience. If you work with them and release them, they will not show up continually when you least expect them, unrepentantly. What are your fears? How can you make friends with them? Once you know what they are, set a clear intention to move through them and not allow them to be a driving force in your life. Squashing them just makes them scream louder.

So if fear is something that plagues you, face it head on, and if needed, get some support to release it. EFT (Transformer 5—Emotional Freedom Technique) can have a very positive effect in releasing fear's grip and then you can fill up the space it leaves with other more positive feelings.

Asking Questions to Get Clear About What I Desire

How clear do you feel about what your future looks like? We will all go through times when we feel like we are floundering, unclear as to the direction we want our life to take. But I have found that asking myself questions is a very easy way to get clear about what I desire and what I want to create in my life.

At one point in my life when I was in a crumbling marriage, I was very unsure of what my next step should be. I knew I was very unhappy and was not in a good place, but old, limiting beliefs just kept me hanging on and trying to resurrect something that had gone sour a long time before.

I asked myself an important question, "Am I here because this is my destiny and where I need to be, or am I afraid to go?" I got the answer very quickly and clearly that I was afraid to go. Making any decision or choice based on fear or lack usually ends up with poor or negative results. Within two months the marriage dissolved and I left.

Questions can be amazing tools, especially when you are open to listening to the answers. Ask yourself, "What do I really want for my life? Is this the right choice for me? What do I need to do to create more peace? Who or what is draining my energy? How do I get out of my own way?" These are just samples. Your questions will be unique to you.

Once you ask the questions, you also have to have the courage to listen to and accept the answers. Sometimes they may not be exactly what you want to hear. Tuning into your intuitive wisdom rather than the mind and allowing it to respond will often get you some surprising answers.

Learn to ask yourself lots of questions and listen to the answers. Sometimes, the answer may not come right away, but you may get an "aha!" later in the day or during the night when your mind is quieter. When you ask questions, also pay close attention to the feelings that come up with the answers. You may feel lightness or a sense of knowing; these confirm that you are on the right track.

Using questions is a great way to get clarity. Setting intent is also very important. The Universe can't give you what you desire if you don't ask for it and set clear intentions. This is the trick—sometimes what you are asking for is not what you actually need. It may be what you want, but not what your highest self requires for your own evolution.

As soon as my marriage ended seventeen years ago, I set a clear intention: I want another relationship with a life partner. Some potential partners showed up temporarily, but now, seventeen years later, I am still single, and the years of being on my own have been so valuable. My learning and growing has come from navigating my life on my own and, though for many years this was a struggle, my life is now a haven where I reside. Being clear is important, but the true motivation behind your intention and what is actually in your highest good will determine what you receive.

How Do You Want to Feel?

Are you communicating with the Universe and telling it what you really want? We need to place much more emphasis on how we want to feel; not about the stuff that we want. All the stuff doesn't matter a hoot if you aren't happy inside. All the stuff in the world isn't going to bring you peace and contentment, if that isn't something you have already cultivated. The positive feelings are the fuel by which we attract what we desire. So that is the first place to start. The reason we want the stuff in the first place is because of how it makes us feel. If, for you, a vacation is about wanting to relax and feel calmer, why not just go for the feeling first?

The **only** reason any of us ever want **anything** is because we think we'll feel better with it than without it. What's the point of feeling awful on the way to getting something?

A while back, I wanted to own a sports car. As I explained earlier, cars have a profound meaning in my subconscious. When I really looked at why I wanted one, it was the feeling of being powerful that the car would provide. So what I was really looking for was the feeling of being powerful and the car was one way to get it. But it was a false sense of power. I did buy the sports car and it was fun to drive, but the personal power came much later and now it doesn't matter what car I drive. True personal power comes from within. If I had felt that I was living in my own power then it wouldn't have mattered what car I had been driving. So why not focus on achieving the feeling first? Then your choices might be very different.

Desiring a good income is about feeling a sense of security and feeling safe in this world. If the feeling is there then it is much easier to manifest the income.

When I was ill with interstitial cystitis, I read a book by Bernie Siegel, M.D. that had a profound effect on me: *Love, Medicine and Miracles*. He said: "Don't focus on healing the illness; just focus on creating inner peace and the rest will follow". I have used this as a mantra for myself ever since. From a place of inner peace, I have created total health and well-being. Yes, I did some physical things differently, such as eating better, taking supplements, and energy work to help with the healing process, but I kept my focus on how I wanted to feel. Once I understood this, the feelings led me to the things I needed to do in order to support my healing and achieve more of those positive feelings.

I had such a clear affirmation of how this works when I took three months off from being a flight attendant; part was paid holidays and part was a leave of absence. At first, I worried about how this would work and whether I had enough savings, blah, blah; but I proceeded. The whole three months was an absolute joy. It was the first time in my life that I had actually taken this amount of time for myself to just be. I planned many trips during this time and all of them went without a hitch. A friend commented, "Wow, you are living the life of the rich and famous!" And it felt like that. That's when it became so clear to me that it is all about how you feel. Feeling good just brought more of the same vibration. At one point, I thought funds were starting to get low and immediately a new client whom I had never met before came along and paid for four sessions in advance. The whole three months was like that. No steady income, but I felt richer than when I was working, and that is because I felt good and was not worried about where money would come from. You feel good, you draw good into your life. Again, like manifests like. Sometimes, it takes more effort to stay positive when life makes demands; but boy, it is worth it!

Start being clear with the Universe on how you want to feel. I am constantly reminding myself that I choose peace, love, joy, happiness, and abundance. These are the states I cultivate every day. It is so easy to let the mind take over and run amok; instead I am adamant about how I want to feel: I want joy in my heart. Then the activities and experiences that you choose will be a mirror of how you want to feel. From this place of peace and joy it is easy to manifest what you desire. You have to be clear and consistent in this intention and practise it every day. In the Transformers chapter, there are numerous tools to help with this endeavour. Pick some to play with and see what works for you.

I also spend a lot of energy cultivating gratitude. I have kept a gratitude journal for almost eighteen years (see Transformer 14—Gratitude Journal).

I have noticed that when I periodically stop journaling, my gratitude life always seems to take a more chaotic turn. Sometimes the chaos affects my ability to find time to journal, but getting right back into journaling helps to overcome the chaos. I do notice that when I keep faithful to this journal, really feeling the gratitude, and not just writing it out, life is much easier, and I am able to avoid getting into the chaos and staying more neutral when life goes amok as it sometimes does. So now I don't even bother taking time away from this practice. I do it every day and keep tabs on my entries by adding them up at the end of each month: if all the entries are filled, I celebrate. I find that when I haven't missed a day, life is usually smooth and when I have, I can reflect back on the month and see that there may have been some challenges and I wasn't as peaceful. The process is so helpful in keeping my "monkey mind" at bay. When I ask what I am grateful for as I write and keep asking what else I am grateful for, I have to think about it. I think my gratitude journal and my focus on feeling grateful is a huge contributing factor to my feelings of contentment.

So how do you want to feel? Make a list of all the feelings that expand your heart. Focus every day on feeling compassion, love, and joy, and not just saying the words but actually feeling them. Let these words actually fill your heart and warm your whole body. Doing Transformer 15—Tapas Acupressure Technique With Affirmations is a great way to get this message even deeper into the brain.

Once you are clear with yourself on how you want to feel and put this into practice, then giving the Universe instructions on what you desire is much easier to manifest. You do need to be clear with the Universe as to what you want. We can be too apathetic about our lives and just let them transpire without really giving clear instructions about what we desire. Ask and you will receive, but don't place any expectations, timelines, or qualifiers; ask, and then let it go, so the Universe can work its magic on your behalf. We keep ourselves limited by not asking. If you are not clear as to what you want your life to look like, you are not being the director of your life and the play you create may not be the one you want.

Think Big Not Small

My friend uses this expression "choose the bigger life" and she sure has accomplished so much in her life. There is also the wonderful quote by Marianne Williamson: "Our deepest fear is not that we are inadequate. Our deepest fear is that we are powerful beyond measure. It is our light, not our darkness, that most frightens us. We ask ourselves: 'Who am I to be brilliant, gorgeous, talented, and fabulous?' Actually, who are you not to be? ...".

We are all part of creation and have the same divine intelligence that created this Universe.

"Your playing small does not serve the world. There is nothing enlightened about shrinking so that other people won't feel insecure around you. We are all meant to shine [and create awesomeness].... It's not just in some of us; it's in everyone. And as we let our own light shine, we unconsciously give other people permission to do the same. As we are liberated from our own fear, our presence automatically liberates others" (Marianne Williamson, www.marianne.com).

We allow ourselves to think small typically out of fear and wanting to conform. What if we are way more than we think we are? What if our potential is way beyond what we presently think? Again, who is doing the thinking? Is it your magnificent self or is it some voice or message from the past that has translated into some negative belief?

Your consciousness may be keeping you in a framework that is limiting. If you opened up to other possibilities and expanded your desires without limitations, what would they be? Think outside the box and reach for possibilities you may not have considered before. Try it on. How does it fit? Does the ego mind come up with all its arguments and negative chatter, like mine did when I wanted to become a flight attendant? Challenge them. Ask your Creator self what it thinks. You may find it smiling and saying, "Go for it!"

Knowing When to Move Your Feet

Action is, surprisingly, the last and least important step in getting what we desire. But most of us have been taught exactly the opposite. We think our action —what we **do**—is what creates the results we get. That's backwards. In fact, most of the action that fills our days seems necessary precisely because we aren't paying attention to our thoughts. We don't really get that we are creating our experience through our thinking, which then results in our feelings, which create what we attract into our lives. Knowing what thoughts are behind your doing will determine what you create. Are your thoughts based in fear or lack, or inspiration and joy?

"Inspired Action Only." Those simple words appear on little sticky notes on my computer, in my car, and elsewhere as reminders to make sure that what I **do** comes from real inspiration, instead of from mere motivation. What's the difference? Inspired action is action taken when everything on the "inside" is so right that the action seems altogether natural, as though it's the obvious next step. You'll just see it clearly and follow it with faith and purpose.

Motivated action is action taken because of outside influences triggering emotions like fear, envy, anger, etc. There's no point in taking any action until you're completely clear on what it is you desire and you are feeling enthusiasm and happiness whenever the thought of it enters your head. Then any action you take will be inspired by that thought and feeling. That's far better than taking action—well-planned or not—that's merely motivated by something else. When you're about to burst with the delicious desire to swing into action, when it seems like "Of course! This is the right thing for me to do right now and I can't wait to get started", then you're on-track.

I still have to keep reminding myself of this because my default mode, as I have said earlier, is doing, and I tend to fly right into this action place and end up wasting time—which I wouldn't have, if I'd just waited until I felt inspired. Sometimes the best "action" is to do nothing. My ego still finds this very hard!

Here's the quick way to tell the difference between inspired action and motivated action. Inspired action: "Wow, I could do this and the results could be fantastic!" Motivated action: "Uh oh. If I don't do this, all these awful things will probably happen." When you are in doubt, wait. If your doing is based on "shoulds", you will just be "shoulding" on yourself. That could just take you to a road you don't really want to go on; it will be a waste of your precious energy. A day or two spent in contemplating the vision of what you want, and in earnest thanksgiving that you are getting it, will bring your mind closer to your inspired self and then you will know what to do next. Remember: There is never any hurry on the creative plane in the Universe. This is the place of unseen potential. So when you find yourself fretting, falling into that stressful, pressured feeling of needing to do something, realize that the feeling is your warning signal that your thinking is actually focused on something you don't want or on the absence of what you do want. It's a sure sign you've fallen into the egoic mind: not where inspired action comes from. And ultimately the results of that kind of thinking and the action that grows out of it can never bring you what you want; not in any lasting, deeply satisfying way. So, when you feel frantically like you need to do something, make space, do nothing except ask for inspiration, and wait. The right answer will come.

In my own language around action, I substitute "creating" for the word "doing." Creating has such a different connotation to it. It is more expansive than doing and it implies imagination and changes the focus. So become a Creator not a Doer.

Of course, before you do any creating you need to be clear on what you are asking for. When you are asking, ask from the heart and mind in unison, not from an ego place. It has to come from a clean, clear, open, and expansive place.

Once you are clear on what you desire, clear the pathway for this to transpire. When I have set an intention for my dreams, I act as if they are already coming. I am unified with them.

So, if it is a new car I desire, I go out and buy something for my new car. Maybe it's a new mat or something to hang from the mirror. I set it aside until the new car arrives. I have always done this. For example when I want a new home, I start packing and putting things I don't need into boxes. I am giving clear instructions that I am on the move. I buy something for this new home and set it aside until I have moved in. It is preparing the way and knowing that this new desire is going to show up. Again, you don't have to know how it will happen, you just have to hold the dream.

Your dream may be a career. When I decided I was going to become a flight attendant, I bought some airplane earrings for my new job which I didn't have—yet. Sure enough, I got to wear them on my new job. I also find that doing this is fun; it's childlike; it's like playing pretend, and honouring the child energy that believes everything is possible, magical, wondrous. It honours that energy to unfold and creates a more positive space for this dream to nurture and grow.

Another message is to show you know you are deserving; be nice to yourself. Treat yourself with love and kindness and respect. Show the Universe that you feel deserving of whatever it is that you desire. Treat yourself to flowers. Say no when someone asks you to do something that doesn't feel right. Make choices that show you value yourself.

Give messages to the Universe that you are aligned with what you desire and then trust that it is on its way.

Keeping Your Dreams Close to Your Heart

I tend to think way outside the box and I create from this place. On the surface, my dreams may look unrealistic in ego terms, but if my heart says "Yes" to something, then I know the Universe will find a way to make it happen. I just have to hold the dream, feel one hundred percent clear around it with no wanting, and, just by holding an open-hearted desire, mountains will move to make my dream happen. I do not have to know how; I just have to hold it close in my heart. I usually keep a picture of my dream in my room where only I will see it, and do lots of imagining and positive feeling around what it is I want. I live as if it actually is happening now, and is true for me. I allow the excitement to wash over me and my heart to fill with joy.

I keep my desires (especially ones that are large and appear "undoable") close to my heart. I don't tell my dream to anyone who may be a naysayer or anyone with linear mind thinking who will not see this as possible for me. I believe these people will only deplete the energy around what I want; their energy will give fuel to my ever-present "monkey mind" that will then create doubt, which clouds the energy around what I seek to create. Other people's constructs of their life may be full of their own BS to the point where, even when they have the best intentions, they will not be able to see your dreams for you in the way that you can. Some people may even try to "help" you by showing you all the things that can go wrong, or how you can be disappointed. They will become mirrors for your own fears and doubts. So, be very choosy with whom you share your dreams. As the proverb says: "do not cast pearls before swine". In other words, if you can't be a hundred percent sure that someone will honour your dreams, don't toss something so valuable in front of them to swallow up.

I only share my big dreams with close friends who will say, "You go, girl," and are one hundred percent behind me. They know and reaffirm all the time that I am an amazing manifester. That's the kind of energy you want around your dreams and desires.

Bending Reality

Now this may take you out of your comfort zone, but I personally have had too many experiences, like my car angel incident, to have any doubt that there are unfathomable forces out there supporting me, and they can have a powerful effect on my human existence. And it's not just me. They're there supporting you too. This is again where the mystical comes in. A good example of bending reality just happened to me recently. It was amazing, and you may chalk it up to coincidence, but my belief is there are no coincidences; there is much more Divine synchronicity to our lives than we can reduce to simply coincidence.

Three of us were flying to Florida to attend a gathering for November 11, 2011: it was to be a special retreat to honour the anticipated changes in the Universe coming in 2012. Two of us were flight attendants and one was my dear friend who was flying on one of my airline passes. We diligently checked the flight loads to find out how many extra seats were available, as we were all flying standby. We chose our flight accordingly and away we went. The night before, we checked again—all looked good; eleven seats were available. In the morning, we got up and my flight attendant friend checked again; she was shocked to see there were no seats available on our connecting flight to Florida. What had happened!

Well, we headed to the airport and got on the first leg of the flight. We were meeting our other friend in Toronto for the connection to Florida. Things weren't looking good and if we didn't get this flight there were no other flights that day and the next day looked scarce too. We would miss a whole day of our gathering or perhaps the whole event that we had all paid for and so much wanted to attend. So I sat there and sent out a "call"—which I frequently do—to all my support team, my angels, and for good measure, I called my dear Irish friend who seems to have a very close connection with this force, and said to her, "Send out your people! We need help!" She lovingly obliged and then, I just let it go. It wasn't easy; often it is not easy—but that does seem to be the key.

We got to the airport for our Florida flight and checked with the airport agents. Sure enough there were no seats available: the flight was full. There had been a delay on another flight and eleven people had been transferred.

We shared this news with our friend whom we'd met in Toronto, and it was looking pretty grim. Two of us were able to fly in the jump seat with the pilots, because we worked for the airline, but that left our friend with no way to get there; I would not leave her alone. My friend, the flight attendant, went aboard for the jump seat in the cock pit. We sat in silence as everyone boarded, almost holding our breath. Everyone in the waiting lounge had boarded when the agent made an announcement: "Two people are missing." I held my breath—could it be? The door to the bridge was already closed and I heard the CSA agent ask, "Can I clear the standbys?" and she motioned for us to run. They opened the door and we got the last two seats on the airplane. We made a dramatic entrance with thumbs up from my friend in the jump seat and all the other flight attendants who knew we were trying to get on the flight. The door shut, the plane backed up, and away we went.

We looked at each other—stunned. Wow! That was dramatic! We thanked those two people, who, for whatever reason, did not show up on time at the gate to make their flight. Reality was bent that day and we got to where we needed to go.

I love the term "bending reality". I had not heard it prior to this event, and now I look for opportunities to bend my reality as we did with this flight. I also look for ways that this has happened and I am always so grateful that I have learned to become a deliberate Creator and a bender of my reality. Sometimes it takes longer than I expect it to, and sometimes I have to get out of my way in a major way, but this is a truth for me and for so many others I know. The stories of so many people I know and have heard of that adhere to this truth and create enormous changes in their lives are too significant to be coincidental. Take my friend, for example, who healed bone cancer and has done some other pretty incredible reality bending that you would think isn't possible, but she has. It's only the egoic mind that thinks it's not possible; your limitless self is capable of creating anything. Sometimes a little help from unseen forces is needed.

So, ask for help! You may feel silly at first but with "smouldering passion", as my Irish friend likes to say, after you ask—miracles can occur.

Chapter 9

Lightening Up

The Fun Factor

I have found the more I focus on making my life fun, the easier it is to get out of my own way. We in the West take ourselves far too seriously. The company that I work for has a philosophy: "Take your job seriously, but not yourself". That's why if you fly with us you will quite often find the staff laughing and joking around with each other, or even cracking jokes to make people laugh or singing a funny song over the PA system, anything to keep it light and make the experience of flying much easier. Some flight attendants do interesting safety demonstrations and make everyone laugh. For a bit, our guests forget about their problems and are present and having fun.

One Christmas I was on my own and knew I wouldn't be seeing any family or friends as I had to work. I thought, "Well, I still need some presents," so I went shopping, but I wanted the gifts to be a surprise. I thought I would pick out a few things that appealed to me and then give them to the salesclerk to choose one or two and wrap them up for me. As I explained this plan to the sales clerk, she looked rather dubious, but then she got right into it. I picked out my presents, she made the choice for me, gave me the parcel, and then winked and said, "Don't peek!" The sales clerk was so happy to help and she wrapped up my surprise for me. I went into another store and did the same thing. On Christmas morning—as I was opening my gifts—I truly was surprised as to what they had picked. There was one item I had especially wanted, and sure enough, it was there. I had had so much fun shopping that day and a wonderful surprise on Christmas morning. This could have been rather a depressing time, but I chose to make it fun.

I have even learned that when I am doing energy work with people, I try to keep it light for myself with an open curiosity as to what will show up. Keeping it light makes it so much easier for me to hear what I need to do.

Humour

Humour has been a very healing force in my life.

It only takes seventeen muscles to smile, but forty three to frown. Smiling is much easier. Dr. Bruce Lipton says in *Spontaneous Evolution*, "Smiling reduces the secretion of stress hormones and raises the production of endorphins, which are the body's natural feel good hormones while simultaneously enhancing the function of the immune system by increasing T-cell production" (page 354). These are very powerful benefits of just smiling.

Dr. Siegel, author of *Love, Medicine and Miracles*, presents the case that a good sense of humour promotes good health: "Laughter is associated with a sense of well-being, which is associated with a strong immune system and quicker recovery from illness or injury".

I have learned a lot about humour from my oldest son and my father. Both have taught me to laugh more, and my son can make me laugh like no one else can. He has a wonderful sense of humour and can see the funny side of even the most difficult situations. He often turns hardships into funny stories that elicit the laugh response. I still save his letters to read when I need a giggle. He always comes out on top because of this amazing attitude, even through some very difficult times like a seven-month posting in Afghanistan where he was chief of combat search and rescue.

Many years ago when I was going through a serious depression, after my marriage had broken up and I was feeling like my world had come to an end, my son flew me out to where he was stationed in Winnipeg, Manitoba. Afterward, we were going to drive home to Ontario. As most of us know, this part of our country is extremely flat. As they say, "you can watch your dog run away for three days".

As we were preparing for the camping trip home we went to stock up on supplies. I went to pick up my usual self-help books, and my son looked at me and said, "You know Mom, I think it's time for something else." He then picked up two large books of the *Calvin and Hobbes* comic book series (incidentally, Calvin definitely reminds me of my son) and we headed out across the flat lands. I spent most of the trip reading to myself or out loud to my son from *Calvin and Hobbes,* and laughing so hard the tears were rolling down my face. One night when we were camping, the wind was so fierce it almost picked up the tent from underneath us, but we just kept reading and laughing. By the time I got near home, I felt lighter and more optimistic and I knew I had left my depression in Manitoba. It was an amazing experience. Humour can be lifesaving. Thank you, James!

Hook is a fantastic movie with Robin Williams as a grown-up Peter Pan who has forgotten who he is. He is caught up with life and not very happy. He ends up back in Neverland and finally discovers that he can fly when he thinks happy thoughts. His happy thought was a thought of his son being born. Happy thoughts are represented by marbles. At the end of the movie, Peter Pan sees one of the lost boys and gives him a bag of marbles. The lost boy is so excited he says, "I thought I had lost my marbles," and with them in hand he is able to fly. I love this movie. Your happy thoughts are what give you freedom. I have placed marbles all over my house—so I do not forget my happy thoughts.

I have a wonderful story about my Dad, who had a terrific sense of humour. He was ninety-three when he died and during his last days, he was quite ill with pneumonia. I had been travelling with my work and had come to the nursing home to feed him, which I had been doing for a while, in between other obligations. I was quite tired. I was pretty sure these were his last few days and thought something very profound was about to happen when he said, "Krisse, I want you to put your hand on your chest." I obliged, thinking, "Wow, what is he going to say?"

Out came, "I want you to stop buying that cheap, shit, cognac you have been buying me and get me the good stuff!"

I cracked up and promised to go to the store the next day and get him good cognac! I never made it, as he died the next day. He kept his sense of funny right to the end. I still tell this story and people always laugh.

Chapter 10

Getting Out of the Way

Getting Out of Your Own Way

So to conclude; getting out of your own way means no longer restricting your freedom in psychological servitude to the whims of the personal ego. It means liberating that freedom to be used in the service of your energy and intelligence, the miraculous part of you that is connected to the powerful creative force that created you in the first place.

How do you get in your own way in the first place? What is it that stands between you and what you desire? What stops you from really living the life you want? Get out your journal or just a piece of paper and make a list of all your de-energizing patterns and habits. Maybe it's complaining at work, or eating food that makes you feel bad, saying yes when you really mean no. Maybe it's a belief that you are not enough. What is it that gets in your way of connecting to your Divine intelligence and the magnificence that you are? Own it all and be clear and honest with yourself. You can't change what you don't know is there.

Once you have your list, make a clear intention to: (1) be aware when you are engaged in these old patterns and (2) to be willing to let them go, one hundred percent. And I mean all of them. You are too precious a gift to the Universe not to let your light shine and be all that you can be. No more thinking small. You owe it to yourself and the people around you to be a beacon of light for us all. You do not have to know how these blocks will be released, you just have to be willing and allow your innate intelligence to help you: it's connected to a much greater power than your small mind. Be kind to yourself and accepting; you will be much more aware of when you are getting in your way. Then you can be guided to let these blocks go. You may be guided to use a particular Transformer to help you move forward. You don't have to know which one; just allow your innate wisdom to go to the one that is in your highest good. You are the only obstacle that stands between you and what you want out of life. So get out of the way and let it all unfold.

I remember Dr. Wayne Dyer saying at a workshop I attended: "Keep doing what you love to the best of your ability. Stop judging and get out of your own way". This line has always stuck with me.

Getting Out of Other People's Way

This was a huge realization for me recently. I have become pretty good about getting out of my own way and tempering the antics of my ego mind, but I hadn't extended this process enough to others and to our planet in general. I realized that sometimes I get in other people's way. Let me explain.

I have one particular friend—let's call her Jane—who has had an amazing past. She created a film festival in Canada and has known many influential and famous people whose pictures on her walls you would recognize. She took this in her stride with no ego involved. She was in a very powerful place and had a list of accomplishments that would take many people more than one lifetime to create.

She had changed careers many years back and had become a minister in the New Thought Movement. In this new role, life seemed to have more challenges and what had been a breeze before seemed to be more of a struggle. On many occasions I expressed concern about her to a close mutual friend. Though I do not tend to worry, I found myself engaging a lot in worry for Jane.

Worrying diminishes energy and is a waste of precious mental resources. I love the line I saw on a card one day: "Worrying doesn't empty tomorrow of its struggles, but empties today of its strength".

I kept chatting to the mutual friend about how I wanted Jane's life to be easier and yet I was giving a lot of feeling energy to all the challenges she was having. One day I caught myself and thought, "Wow, I am actually getting in the way of her success by all this focus on her challenges." I shared this with her and she agreed. She had decided that she wanted to make a shift, see herself as successful, and leave these struggles behind. She needed my support to also see her this way. I made a conscious intention to just see her as strong, accomplishing what was really in her highest good. I got out of her way and saw her realize her dreams.

A couple of years back, my eldest son was deployed to Afghanistan and I could feel my ego and my worrywart start to jump in. I decided to not get on this bus and find ways to let it go and do what I could to keep him safe and protected. I went and got many little gifts that all depicted this energy, like an angel ring that said "protection" on it. I gave these to him with my love to keep in a keepsake bag. Even the process of collecting all these items put me in a positive frame of mind, knowing I was putting all my energy into holding him safe. I continued to see him this way every day while he was away. I also didn't watch TV news, so I wouldn't have images of the danger he was in clouding my positive thoughts. I am very grateful that he came home safely and my attitude while he was there stayed positive, so I got out of both our ways to make it easier for us both.

One of my travel companions shared a story of how her mother had been so worried about her travelling to Thailand with a group of friends whom her mom did not know. She was clear with her mom: "Don't put this black cloud of negative energy and fear around me", and had to consciously detach from this energy drain.

I think we do a disservice to those we love by worrying about them or focusing on their problems. We need to see them as strong and able to realize all their dreams. We need to support their choices, even if we may not agree with them. Keep your energy focused on the positive and add strength to them. Don't weaken them by focusing on their problems or the possible challenges they may encounter. If you really want to help those you love, then see them having positive outcomes in their lives and reaffirm this for them even during their most challenging times. When my son was in Afghanistan, I focused on a positive outcome and saw him strong and able to deal with all the challenges he was going to face. I don't know how much it helped him, but it certainly kept me in a sane space.

We are all connected: we breathe the same air and come from the same source of creation, so what you want for others you are also returning to yourself. I have always kept the truth close to my heart that when I help others I am also helping myself. The opposite is also true: if I harm others, I am also harming myself.

So look at how your energy and thoughts are affecting those around you. The more positively you can think about others, the more room there is for their energy to vibrate at a higher frequency and, in return, come back to you.

Ask your friends and the people you love what their dreams are and see those dreams as active in their lives. Doing this will also speed up your own dreams coming to fruition.

My friend David suggests we have "dream buddies" who will affirm our intentions and send us reassuring messages and inspirational quotes to keep the energy around our dreams high. I am his dream buddy and a hundred percent behind him accomplishing his "big dream".

I used to work with families who had children with disabilities. I was amazed at how some of my families were able to hold a vision for their children. When they believed that they could accomplish more than the doctors expected, then this energetically built up the child's potential. If you see and feel that they can move beyond where they are, then they can. If you focus on the disability and what they can't do, then they are being defined by their disability.

Having faith in our realization of the limitless possibilities for ourselves and others will help us all create better lives for ourselves.

If you see others as strong and vibrant you will also see yourself this way. The more we can get out of other people's way, the more we will get out of our own way.

Get Out of the Way of Our Planet

This same principle applies to our thoughts about our planet. Yes, our world is going through a major transition and, yes, there is lots of chaos. Mother Earth has certainly been retaliating against how we have treated her. Talking and putting feeling energy into how challenging things are only holds and magnifies that energy. We need to stop looking for catastrophe. This is one of the reasons I seldom watch the news, as I don't want to have evidence of the world in flux right in my face. We need to see our planet as healing and not ailing. This will be the turning point of collective consciousness and will help to restore balance, bringing peace into our world.

Gregg Braden talks about a study that was done in Israel. They trained a group of people to feel peace in their bodies and at appointed times on specific days, these people were positioned throughout the war-torn areas of the Middle East. During the windows of time when they were feeling peace, terrorist activities ceased and crime went down.

"When a small percentage of the population achieved peace within themselves, it was reflected in the world around them. For example in a city of one million the number is about 100. In the world of 6 billion it's just fewer than 8,000. This calculation represents only the minimum needed to begin the process. The more people involved in feeling peace, the faster the effect is created."

So let's also get out of Mother Earth's way. Help her heal by sending her loving energy. Envision her healing and restoring herself. This starts by our being peaceful ourselves. We all need to take this on with gusto. We need to fill up our hearts with love for our planet and bring this energy to the very core of our existence. Allow this feeling, not the negative, to expand.

Our human potential to manifest this healing energy is immense. It is a choice and one we all need to make. As Ghandi said: "Be the change you wish to see in the world." It begins with us. Feeling helpless and unable to change things adds stress to our lives and bodies, and it is so far from the truth. The only thing that can make a difference in the world is you.

Road Map to Getting Out of Your Own Way

We have covered a lot of ground, so I want to help you with a road map to guide you in getting out of your own way.

1. **First, practise self-awareness:** When you are in the grips of the ego and feel like you are in a negative place, remember you are not lost; you are just exploring. It's just part of the journey.

2. **Second, accept where you are:** Be gentle and kind with yourself and accept where you are, and then if needed, go to the Transformers section and clear the negativity as best you can. So be kind to yourself and keep an open mindset that this is just temporary. You will move through it much more easily with kindness to yourself.

3. **Then work on releasing what is in your way:** Challenge your stinking thinking and make a commitment to yourself to release it so you can create space for miracles. Use the Transformers in this book as tools to help get you there.

4. **Keep your energy clean:** Do some kind of exercise each day, such as Transformer 9—Positive Position, and set a clear intention on how you want to feel. Be clear on what kind of day you want to have. This makes it much easier to stay on track and prevent the ego from getting a grip.

5. **Keep it simple and connect to your Divine God Self:** Cut out the excess noise in your life. Stop watching images or listening to ideas that fill your head with ego fears. Keep your world as peaceful as you can. Playing gentle music helps to calm the mind. Taking time to be in nature is a wonderful way to get connected back to your Divine self. From this place, it is easier to listen to the still voice. Pray, meditate, talk to your wise self, do whatever it takes to stay connected to this powerful force within you.

6. **Love Your Self:** Remember to pack your bag of self-compassion, and be loving and accepting of yourself. It is much easier to journey from this place of kindness to one's self and so much easier to be kind to others when you are filling your own cup up first.

When we truly realize our limitless potential to our very core and feel that miraculous potential that we all have vibrating deep within us, we realize that anything is possible, if only we are willing to get out of our own way. So be inspired by your own life and run it on inspiration. As my angelic friend Denise Hagan says, "Follow the Love."

Chapter 11

Transformers to Create Space for Miracles

Introduction

The following activities are wonderful tools to release old energy and keep your energy free, clean, and clear. I have used all these Transformers on myself and my clients, with great success. I suggest you read over them all so you have them in your memory. Sometimes it is difficult when you are experiencing challenges to know which one to use. I have put these Transformers each on its own page, so when you feel you need some support you can just intuitively open the book to a page and your inner knowing will pick the right Transformer for you to use. Instant therapy! I have had some pretty compelling evidence in my own life and also with many clients about the massive changes that can happen by just using acupressure and other energy techniques to move stagnant energy, which brings about significant and subtle changes to affect a shift.

Following is a lot of information that may be unfamiliar to you and feel somewhat awkward, like attempting to learn a new dance. Learning to do things a new way sometimes makes you feel like a child learning to walk. Changing your behaviour can be a time of transition and sometimes this can have its own challenges. It is so worth it. Play with these tools and see what works for you. Call on your inner child and let it be playful with what you're learning. Don't make it all serious business. Notice which Transformers affect a change and which ones you resonate with. Using your intuition to find which one you need can be fun and it can be interesting to see what comes up for you. What does it say about what is going on for you at the time? Reflect on the ones you seem to be choosing. Are they the same or different? Is there a pattern? Play with it.

A word of caution. Whenever you change your behaviour, it has an effect on those around you. So you may also expect some fallout from friends, families, co-workers, and partners. The people who are closest to you in your life will be the most affected by your change in behaviour, and change in energy.

I remember when I first started to meditate I placed a sign on my bedroom door that said, "Please do not disturb". Shortly after posting this sign, I was in a deep meditative space, blissfully contemplating nothing, when there came a loud knock on my door. It jolted me and I asked, "What's wrong?" I was expecting a crisis of some kind. The reply was, "Telephone for you!" I got up rather annoyed at being disturbed for a telephone call when a message would have done. I announced to my then-partner to please only come and get me if there was blood or if the kids needed help. He was confused and rather annoyed since I was usually right there to attend to others' needs. But, a while later there appeared another sign, this time on his office door: "Please do not disturb", and he started to meditate too. He had witnessed the positive effects of my new practices and saw how much calmer and happier I was. He figured he could also use some of this.

This may not always be the case and you may find others balking at the changes you are making. So stay true to yourself and do what feels right. Let others adjust to your new behaviour and attitude, and be compassionate with them as they adjust.

You may also want to use these Transformers as a preventive routine to help you stay more balanced and centred. I have used these in varying forms for twenty years and continue to do so. I know that these tools have contributed greatly to my contentment today. They will also support you in energizing your entire system to deal better with life.

How do you know when a Transformer has worked? You may feel a deepening of your breath or take a big sigh. You may get a feeling as though you have just landed in your body. You may yawn many times. There are numerous changes that can occur when there has been a shift in our energy. Yours will be unique to you. Just take a moment to notice what happens for you.

A side note: If you choose to do any of these techniques with others, make sure your own energy is fairly clean and keep your mind as empty as you can with no expectations of results. Expectation just gets in the way. If you are working through this book with a partner or friend, make sure the person you're working with is fairly open and clear, and that their energy isn't swirling in a negative place. When I work with others, I tend to go into an altered state and lead from my heart so my mind doesn't get in my way. From this place, I step into the quantum field where anything is possible and all kinds of wonderful information can come flowing to me.

Have Fun!

Transformer 1-Breathing

This Transformer elicits the relaxation response. It helps your mind let go and your body soften and relax.

Taking deep, slow, long breaths is a very quick stress release and can be done anywhere at any time. Breathe in through your nose and bring the air deep into your belly, not just your chest. Feel your breath fill up your belly right up to your chest. You may want to place your hands on your belly and as you breathe in, feel your belly expand and your hands move apart. Then as you exhale, your fingers will again touch. When breathing out, ensure that all the air is out. Typically the outbreath is twice as long as the inbreath. You may want to count quietly to yourself as you are breathing, to take the focus away from the rambling mind. For example, count to 10 on the inbreath and then 20 on the exhale. This can also be coupled with positive self-affirmations, for example, "With this inbreath, I bring in peace and harmony and with this outbreath, I release any and all tensions in my body and mind."

When to Use This Transformer

Breathing deeply can be a great way to start the day and get yourself centred. It is also very helpful in releasing the day's tensions and assisting you get to sleep at night. Use this simple technique anytime you feel the need to refocus and get into a more positive space.

Time to slow down and take a deep breath!

Transformer 2—Meditation

Meditation is a powerful tool for accessing higher intelligence and freeing up the mind from all its incessant chatter. It opens the doors to Divine intelligence/Creation/Source that you would not necessarily have by simply accessing the mind. Many people are daunted by meditation because they feel it means you must have no thoughts. This is not the case. Thoughts will be there as you meditate, but you are not attached to them and you can just let them pass like birds flying by. Just notice them but remain detached from any feelings or emotion they evoke. Don't let them sidetrack you. Sometimes, you may find they decrease considerably through just noticing them, but this is not always the case and that's okay. Meditation will be unique to you and your experience of it. Using the breath as described earlier is a way to get your body into the more relaxed state that supports meditation.

I have meditated for about eighteen years and I try to stay pretty consistent with it. Meditation does not always have to be the traditional form of just sitting quietly and emptying the mind, which isn't always easy. It can also be active, like walking, and just being in tune with nature and your surroundings. Eating a piece of chocolate cake with absolute focus and awareness can be a form of meditation—I personally like this one! Just sitting for five or ten minutes and watching your thoughts can be a form of meditation. Any time you simply stop your egoic mind from racing and place your focus on your connection to yourself is a meditation.

When to Use This Transformer

Meditation is a Transformer that can be used on a regular basis to clear the mind and create self-awareness. I tend to meditate most mornings and then do a short meditation in the evening before I go to sleep. Play with it and see what works for you. This is a Transformer that, if used regularly, can have a huge impact on helping you gain clarity and insight by quieting your mind.

Release the external world and go inward!

Transformer 3—Scripting a New Story

This is one of my favourite transformers; I use it quite frequently.

Scripting a New Story means pretending that what you want is already here, writing it out and celebrating it with words like, "That's right! I am so excited that this has shown up in my life".

If the new story is about a relationship, then write how it feels to have this relationship in your life. What is it like to go out for dinner and hold hands and feel support from each other? The more details you give the more it seems to come alive, which creates a pathway for that experience to come into your life. Your energy is already connected to the energy of a relationship. The more you feel that what you desire is true for you, the easier it is for this to show up.

If it's a trip you want to take, then write how it feels to be in the place you want to go to. Imagine it in every detail. Feel the feelings; really get into them. I find this such an uplifting exercise. Then, to make it even stronger, you can share your dream with a friend who can mirror it back to you. Your friend can say, "Wow! Isn't it wonderful that this has happened for you!" She can affirm it for you as if it had already taken place. It's amazing how much power this can have in bringing a desire into actual creation. If you do not have someone to share it with, or you choose not to, then reading it back to yourself in front of the mirror also works well. Really immerse yourself in the positive feeling energy. That is where the magnetic force to draw what you desire comes from.

When to Use This Transformer

This is a great exercise to do when you want to start something new, like a new business, or you want to create a new relationship. It also helps you get clarity as to what you want to manifest in your life. How does this feel in your life? You may find that after you imagine it in all its glory, it doesn't fit with what you truly desire, and that's a great revelation. You can then free up energy for something else that does serve you well, and manifest that into existence. I never start a new project without scripting it first. The Universe can't bring something to us unless we are clear what it is.

Articulate your dreams! What do you really want for your life.

Transformer 4—Emotional Stress Release (ESR)

Important: never use pressure; always make sure your touch is light as a feather.

Emotional stress release—ESR—is a very effective technique and one of my favourite Transformers. For example if anger is a trigger, doing an ESR can be a very powerful release. Or, you can try using your intuitive wisdom by opening up to a page in this section to see which Transformer would be best for you. This is an amazing tool that I have used with clients and workshop participants hundreds of times and always with positive results. Each time I've used it, the issue at hand disappears and the participant is calm once again.

This can be effectively done on your own, but through experience, I have found this much more powerful when the points are held by someone else.

Doing This on Your Own

Lie on your back and place your middle fingers on the frontal eminences (the bony protrusions above your eyeballs in the centre of your forehead). Place your thumbs as far down the side of your face in front of your ears as you can and your index fingers rest on the top of your head on the vertex (fontanelle or soft spot). Now think of the problem or issue you are having and rate it on a scale of 0-10, where 10 is the most stressful and 0 not stressful at all. Then think of the problem, focus on every aspect of it, and just stay with these thoughts and feelings.

Doing it on someone else

Have the person decide what issue they would like to work on. They don't even need to tell you what it is. Get them to score it as above. Have them sit on a comfy chair with you behind them. Place your middle fingers on the frontal eminences of their forehead, your index fingers on the side of the head in front of the ears, and your thumbs on the vertex on the top of the head. Hold this position, and breathe slowly and evenly yourself, remembering to empty your mind and send healing energy to your friend. Periodically check in with your friend to see how they are feeling. Hold it until your friend notices that the issue has dissipated.

When to Use This Transformer

Use this any time you want to release an issue that has become an emotional trigger. Once the trigger is released and you aren't emotionally reacting to the issue/problem, then a solution is easier to come by. Then you can let go of the stress and relax into it.

When I was doing my corporate work, I had a workshop participant come up as I demonstrated ESR to the group. She exemplified how effective the technique is. As I held the ESR acupressure points for her, I asked her how she was feeling and she said, "That issue is long gone; I'm on to another problem." We laughed and moved on to the next person.

Something is bothering you. You are playing this story over in your mind. Time to let it go.

Transformer 5—Emotional Freedom Technique (EFT)

Emotional Freedom Technique is one way to reprogram the brain and get control of unsupportive mental scripts. EFT is a psychological acupressure technique.

The process includes tapping acupressure points, while saying affirmations and breathing deeply one breath per affirmation. It is described below in detail. Choose an issue that is bothering you, or doesn't support your highest good. Then create an affirmation that re-patterns that issue. For example, if eating is your issue, affirm to yourself, "My body only desires food that is healthy and supports my system in every way." Put as much emotion and emphasis as you can in what you're saying. This way your affirmations will get anchored in your brain. You can find many how-to videos on the internet to show you specifically what to do. Just google "Emotional Freedom Technique".

EFT can help you:

- Remove negative emotions;
- Reduce food cravings;
- Reduce or eliminate pain; and
- Implement positive intentions.

It is a very powerful tool for transformation, especially if you feel you have "tried everything", and still need to shift things energetically.

How to do an EFT

a. Determine what to say:
When doing EFT, you need to honour what the issue is and include it in your affirmation. If we deny the underlying problem and look only for relief from its symptoms, it just drives the problem deeper into our subconscious; it is still there waiting to jump out at us when we least expect it. Best to acknowledge the truth and bring it to the forefront, so you can then dance with it, and put it behind you.

Here is what you could say to yourself:

"Even though I still have this (fear of public speaking, headache, anger toward my father, war memory, craving for junk food, stiffness in my neck, lack of financial resources, or whatever the issue is that you would like to change), I deeply and profoundly love, honour, and accept myself." Or you can use any praise that you are comfortable with that brings acceptance and love.

Another option is the choice method. This can be used for specific issues in combination with the above self-affirmation, or once the self-affirmation is lodged in your brain. For example:

"Even though I am still anxious about this new job, I choose to know that I am confident and secure in my abilities to do it well."

Acknowledge what the problem or fear is, and then reverse it. Change it to how you want to feel so you can then manifest that feeling, instead of the problem or fear.

b. Solidly tap the following acupressure points:

Using your three middle fingers, start with the karate chop point on the side of either hand or tap with the other hand. As you tap, say your affirmation. Remember to breathe deeply with each affirmation. Then move through the following acupressure points, using both hands on both sides:

- The soft spot on the top of your head (only one hand needed);
- At the eyebrows (on the inside, right at the edge of the eyebrow);
- Sides of temples (on the soft spots beside the outside corner of your eyes);
- On the centre of the cheekbones just below your eyes;
- Under your nose;
- Under your lip;
- In the middle of your upper chest (thymus area);
- Below your collar bones (the soft spot right under your collar bones and beside your sternum).

As you move along the points, leave out any negativity (i.e., "Even though I have anger", "a lack of financial resources", or whatever it is) and just focus on the positive outcome. If it's money, affirm. "Wow, I see all this money flowing into my account. I don't have to know how, but I feel it coming. Wow, this feels great. I am receiving money easily."

If the issue still persists but has lessened, honour that in your affirmation by using the word "some". For example, "Even though I still have some of this [whatever it is], I totally love honour and accept myself." This acknowledges that there is a decrease in the problem.

I'd like to share a story around EFT in connection with some volunteer work I did at a local prison in the early 2000s. We called ourselves the Self-Studies Growth Group. This was a medium-security prison and it was a harsh reality that these inmates lived in. They were serving sentences for a variety of reasons, even for murder. What they had in common was their willingness to take responsibility for what they had done and to change their lives by looking inside themselves.

On one occasion, I planned to teach them EFT. Everyone was willing and we had about sixteen guys attend that night. We had to find something in common so we could all do the EFT together. We came up with the word "Lonely". I had just lost my Dad and certainly felt acutely lonely, which was something the guys all shared too. We went through the process as described above and we did it aloud. I could feel the tears on my own face as we proceeded and saw this reflected in the faces around me. We were in a circle and the healing energy was palpable. When we were done there was a softness in their faces that I hadn't seen before and everyone just sat there. We were amazed at what had taken place. I will never forget that experience of healing and how profound these techniques can be.

When to Use This Transformer

This is a really valuable Transformer in developing acceptance of one's self and creating more self-esteem. It is also helpful in changing limiting patterns and creating new circuits of thought around old beliefs. It seems to take the trigger away from an issue and to soften its grip, which allows you to expand your thinking around an issue. It is great with setting intentions and manifesting them. If you feel there are still some old blocks in the way of an intention you want to create, then do EFT around it and see it shift.

Free yourself from limitations. Tap your way to freedom.

Transformer 6—Time to Make Room for Fun

Take time to play. What makes you feel giddy like when you were a kid? Read a funny book, or see a funny movie and laugh. Do something silly with friends and have fun! Tap into your inner kid and just play.

Time to make room for fun.

Transformer 7—Make a Love List

This is a powerful tool to keep you focused on high vibrational thoughts. Focus on what you love. Maybe it's your children or grandchildren, taking trips, or sitting in front of the ocean just staring at the water. Whatever it happens to be, write it all down. You could even get some pictures that depict what you love and make a collage out of them. Keep this list or collage where you can see it as a reminder of what is really important to you. When you see this list, feel those feelings of love you have for those people, places or things, and feel your energy increasing as you focus on what fills your heart with love. The more you focus on what you love, the more it will show up in your life. Make sure you are number one on that list!

When to Use This Transformer

This is a powerful Transformer to use when the ego has taken over and you find yourself focusing on the negative. This can bring you back to focus on what really matters to you.

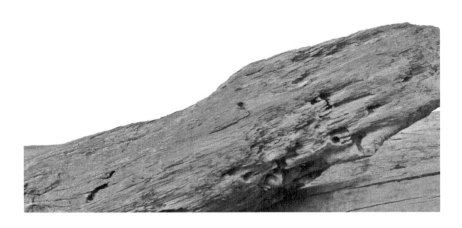

What are you passionate about? What fills your heart?

Transformer 8—Ho'oponopono

This is a powerful transformer and one I use frequently. It is my "go to" in helping me to release old junk and return to my peace. It is a cleansing tool from Ho'oponopono. I have added to the line with a statement that I have found says it all and helps me to move on quickly and release the emotion or judgment.

I had a situation recently when I felt I was not being valued. A family member was triggering this and I felt old anger arising, a rare emotion for me. I could feel myself steaming up inside so I took some "time out" and started repeating this set of lines over and over. Within five minutes, I could feel the anger totally dissipate and I was peaceful once more; I could continue with our family outing with ease and grace. I was again reminded how powerful this tool is.

This is the tool: "I am sorry for the erroneous thoughts that have created this judgment [or anger, or whatever the situation is that you are experiencing]. Please forgive, thank you, I love you. Now there is only innocence and I join my Divine self and choose peace." The statement about innocence reaffirms to our self that we were once a "clean slate" and free of the encumbering beliefs or emotions that we have taken on from our external world; and choosing peace is our choice. I find my body immediately relaxes when I repeat this and it's like my Divine self is so grateful that this is my choice.

Use this whenever you are in judgment or triggered by another. It is one of the most powerful tools in getting out of your own way!

You are being triggered by others.
It is time to cleanse and forgive and release!

Transformer 9—Positive Position - Brain Gym term "Hook-ups"

This is also part of the Bliss Method, but it is great to use on its own. It is such a valuable tool to de-stress the body and give you time out. It can be done anywhere, and it will help you attain balance and centring. It is a great way to start the day.

Go somewhere quiet to sit (or you can sit at your desk at work).

Cross your ankles and place your right arm over the left arm with palms facing down.

Clasp your hands and then draw them underneath to your chest. (Like giving yourself a warm hug.)

Sit for five minutes and just take deep breaths. Place your tongue on the roof of your mouth (which connects to your central meridian).

You can also use this time to say positive things to yourself, like "I am relaxed and calm" or whatever works for you to make you feel better.

When to Use This Transformer

If you don't have time to meditate and all you have is five minutes in the morning to create some "me-time", then the Positive Position is a good choice to use as a regular focusing exercise. It is also good to use this position if you are doing affirmations, just about any time you want to rebalance yourself.

Your mind is ruling you! It is time to integrate and calm yourself.

Transformer 10—Materialize and Dematerialize

List three things—objects, resources, opportunities, or people—that you would like to materialize in your life. Then list three things that you are ready to let go of, that you would like to dematerialize, like excess weight, an addiction, clutter, or a limiting pattern.

Focus on the three items on your materializing list one by one and imagine having each; really feel each of them, and all the details. Let your body get excited and keep investing attention and imagining until your body can feel its presence as normal. Then let go and move on to the next one.

When you are finished, imagine how your life feels now that all three items are a normal part of your reality. How have you grown?

Next look at the items on your dematerializing list one by one. Focus attention on the first one. It's a normal part of your reality. Pull your attention out of it. If it is still a trigger you can do an ESR around it to release its hold. Stop resisting it and let yourself feel bored and uninterested. Does the item have a symbolic meaning or an emotional tie? Let it fade. Let yourself feel unmotivated concerning it. Let yourself feel appreciation for what it has given you, bless it and send it on its way. You don't have to take action now: just release it and dissolve it in your mind. Then let it go. Do the same for the others on your list.

Imagine what your life feels like with these items gone from your reality, replaced by fresh space for new things. Now, that's expansion.

When to Use This Transformer

This is helpful when you feel you are needing to move forward and clear old energy, take a new direction, or when you really want to anchor your new intentions and open up more space for them.

Time to lighten up your life and let go what doesn't fit any more;
manifest new expressions in your life.

Transformer 11—Three Heart Energy Exercises

A) Heart Lock-In®

Five Simple Steps:

1. Close your eyes and relax. Do deep breathing.
2. Shift your attention away from the mind to the area around your heart. If it helps you to focus, put your hand on your heart. Visualize your breath going in and out through the area of your heart and take very slow, deep breaths.
3. Now, find something that's easy for you to appreciate: your partner, your children, or the many good things in your life. Send them genuine appreciation and love for five minutes as you breathe through your heart (or longer, if convenient, for extended benefits). Really feel the emotion of appreciation, not just the thought.
4. As you catch your mind wandering, gently bring your focus back to the heart, and continue sending appreciation and love.
5. After you've finished doing the Heart Lock-In®, try to sincerely sustain those feelings of appreciation and love as long as you can. This will act as a cushion against recurring stress or anxiety.

B) Dropping Into the Heart

In your mind, imagine going down a waterslide and dropping into your heart, or you can imagine taking an elevator to the heart area and stepping off the elevator on the "heart floor". While you are imagining this, place both your hands in front of your face, palms facing to the floor and slowly push the energy into your heart area, then keep your focus on your heart. Dropping into the heart before you meditate is helpful for keeping your focus away from the mind and its ramblings. For anyone in the helping profession, this is a good exercise to do so that you are coming from a heart space when working with others.

C) Heart Expansion Exercise

Get into a comfortable place and if needed to help you relax, have some soft gentle music playing in the background. Take many deep breaths and drop into your heart using the exercise above. Just imagine a force of light as powerful as the sun deep in your heart area. Now, feel this grow and extend throughout your whole body. Once your heart is open, expanded, and full of this light, imagine how open it is to receiving! Feel this heart energy open to receiving all good.

When to Use These Transformers

Use any of these heart Transformers before meditating to bring you into more of a heart space. If you do any healing work (or any profession for that matter), I think it is imperative to come from this loving space before you work with anyone. If you have an issue around holding any resentment toward anyone, taking yourself into your heart will help soften this so you can release old hurts. Maybe you need to be more loving toward yourself. Then take yourself to your heart area and share this loving energy with yourself.

Transformer 12—Vitality Point

For this Transformer, it is better if you are lying down.

Take your thumb and press two finger lengths below the belly button. A firm strong pressure is needed. It helps you to revive when in a weakened state. This is a very powerful tool and it is easy to do. Again this can be more powerful when done by another.

When to Use This Transformer

Use this when you are feeling sick or just feeling low. If you feel you are coming down with something, this could help prevent you from getting sick. It will help to bring vitality and energy back into the body and is also very helpful for back pain. It softens all the muscles in the lower back and releases tension, thereby lessening back pain. It also strengthens the immune system.

This was an extremely valuable tool for me when I was ill.

Time to reenergize your physical body.

Transformer 13—Meridian Wash

A meridian wash follows the lines of the meridians in the body to help clear any blocks and to clean out any static energy in them. This is a great prevention tool to use to keep you balanced. It takes just a few minutes. Stand with your feet apart on the floor and follow the tracing pattern below with both your hands. You are not touching the body, but moving energy along these lines. Do it as slowly as you can to really get the effect. The numbers beside the meridians are the beginning and end points of that meridian.

TRACING PATTERN	MERIDIANS AFFECTED
Down the front: From eyes to toes.	**Stomach** (1 to 45)
Up the front of the body: From toes to top of torso.	**Spleen** (1 to 21)
Down the inside of the arms.	**Heart** (1 to 9)
Up the outside of the arms to the face.	**Small Intestine** (1 to 19)
Down the back: From eyes over top of the head to the toes.	**Bladder** (1 to 67)
Up the front: From toes to top of torso.	**Kidney** (1 to 27)
Down the inside of the arms.	**Circulation/Sex** (1 to 9)
Up the outside of the arms to the face.	**Triple Warmer** (1 to 23)
Down the sides: From eyes to the toes.	**Gall Bladder** (1 to 44)
Up the front: From toes to top of torso.	**Liver** (1 to 14)
Down the inside of the arms.	**Lung** (1 to 11)
Up the outside of the arms to the face.	**Large Intestine** (1 to 20)
Place one hand palm facing down in the front of the groin area and the other palm facing up in the base of your tailbone. Move the energy up until both hands meet at above and below your lip. When moving your hand up the back you have to shift your arm and rotate it and you will miss a bit, but that is okay.	**Three times**
Up the back midline: Over the head to the top of the mouth. Do this simultaneously with "Up the front midline", described below.	**Governing** (1 to 28)
Up the front midline: To the bottom of the mouth. Do this simultaneously with "Up the back midline", described above.	**Central** (1 to 24)

When to Use This Transformer

As mentioned, this is a powerful prevention tool to keep your energy clean and clear. It can be done in the morning to create better energy for the day or in the evening to release any stagnant energy you have carried over from the day.

Time to look beyond the present
and see what is really possible for yourself.

Transformer 14—Gratitude Journal

This is a practice I have maintained for almost twenty years. The few times that I have let myself wane this practice, I always notice that stuff seems to go haywire and I get right back to this practice. It feels good, and when I feel good, my life is good! It's very simple. Every day, I just write what I am grateful for in a special journal I keep just for this purpose. It is a simple tool, but I think very meaningful. It keeps your energy focused on the good you already have, which builds an energy around you that you are grateful and accepting of all the good in your life. My moments of gratitude are simple: sometimes I am grateful that I've had a productive day, or that I get to spend time with my grandchildren, or for the beautiful sunset I saw. It can be anything. Remember to really connect to what you're expressing gratitude for and feel those good feelings. The more you evoke the feeling of gratitude when journaling your gratitude, the more powerful this Transformer can be.

When to Do This Transformer

I recommend doing this daily. You will be surprised at how life will change. If every day isn't possible, do it as often as you can and just notice what life is like on the days you "count your blessings".

Time to switch gears and focus on gratitude.

Transformer 15—Tapas Acupressure Technique With Affirmations

Place your thumb and ring finger of one hand (either will do) on your inner eye points, roughly 1/8 inch above the inner points of the eyes. Rest your middle finger on your third eye (in the centre of your forehead, between your eyes). The rest of your fingers can rest on your face. With the other hand, cover the back of your skull and let your thumb rest on the lower skull line, as if you were cradling your head.

State affirmations that work for you. Do this for as long as you feel good and then switch hands and repeat.

Here are some examples of affirmations:

- I am free, clean, and clear.
- I am an open receiving vessel for all good.
- I am at one with the source that created me.
- I am abundance, joy, and peace.
- I am limitless and know I am totally supported by Creation (God).
- I am so excited about life and enjoy its unfolding.
- I allow life to live through me and not in spite of me.
- I flow with my life.

Create your own, what works for you.

When to Use This Transformer

Do this Transformer any time you want to reinforce affirmations.

Set a clear intention for your life and tap into a new reality.

Transformer 16—Spirit Action

This is an amazing tool to help you stay focused on what really matters and to keep compassion and kindness alive in your consciousness. I put a line in my gratitude journal each day that says "Spirit Action", and think of an action I can take daily to act from my heart/spirit. This is a reminder to act from spirit and do something kind for another person or for our planet. Some people would call this practising "random acts of kindness". It could be bringing flowers to a nursing home for someone who doesn't get many visitors, giving money to the homeless, giving small gifts to women's shelters, like socks or mitts, or sending a kind email to someone telling them how much I value them. Genuinely compliment someone like a cashier. Tell people they are doing a good job. It can be anything that warms your heart and feels good. It takes us out of ourselves when we reflect on someone else's needs rather than our own. You'll raise their spirits, and in turn, raise your own. Again, when we help others we help ourselves.

When to Do This Transformer

This is a good exercise to do every day if you can, to keep you focus positively outside yourself and to keep you feeling good. Anytime you feel you are too involved in your own woes and need to refocus and get out of yourself and your own worries, spirit action will help. It's a great way to get perspective on what's really important, and the bonus is that you'll brighten up someone else's day too.

Focus on helping others and expressing random acts of kindness.

Transformer 17—Practise Being Happy

Take a deep breath in and close your eyes. Just say to yourself, "I am happy," allowing yourself to really feel the happy feelings. Start a smile, even if you have to "fake it till you make it". It will help to get those positive feelings going. If you need extra help to get there, think of a time that made you happy.

For me it's quite often times with my grandson when we are having our Cole/Mummu Adventures.

What do you notice? Did your lips curl up just a little? If so, you just changed the chemistry in your brain. Just stay with this feeling and practise being happy.

When to Use This Transformer

You can practise being happy anytime you feel negative thoughts creeping in, or just want to be happier!

Time to change your inner landscape and find what makes you happy.

Transformer 18—Daily Abundance Log

This exercise helps with attuning the mind to prosperity. Keep a daily log of when abundance has shown up in your life. This doesn't have to be in monetary ways; it can be when someone pays you a compliment or shows love and kindness to you. It can also be material, like someone giving you money, or paying for your lunch, or getting a really good deal on something you buy. Celebrate these experiences and more of them will show up.

When to Use This Transformer

This one is good to use when you want to draw more abundance to your life, whether it is a financial matter or simply some positive experiences.

Change your focus to what is good in your life!

Transformer 19—Bliss Method

This is a lengthier routine that I first read about in Maryam Webster's *Every Day Bliss for Busy Women*. It can take up to five to ten minutes depending how long you want or have time for. The longer you do it, the deeper the effects. I do this some mornings before I leave my bedroom. There is a better chance I will get it done this way.

1. Rub/scrub around the vertex (this is the soft spot on the top of your head) in a circular motion with all your fingers (like in a loose fist), clockwise direction, ten times. This opens the crown to receiving new energy to power your day.

2. Interlace fingers on the centre of your forehead and then pull your hands apart firmly and slowly toward the ears, five times.

3. With a good firm pressure, thump the soft spots right under your clavicles and then the thymus area of the breastbone in the upper chest. Do this to the rhythm of saying, "In love with me, in love with me." Then tap the liver points that are under the breast in line with the nipples, and the spleen points (use a thumping with both arms like you were doing the chicken dance). These are the "ouch" points under the armpits (about four inches down). Tap under the arms. Lastly, do the lymph rub with your fist in a circular motion (this one you do more gently); these are the sore spots on the upper chest, just above the breasts; they are two of the neurolymphatic drainage points. Repeat ten times for each acupressure point, for three repetitions. Do the cross crawl as follows. In a standing position, move your left elbow to touch your right knee, moving your whole body in that direction. Then, go in the opposite direction. (If this is not possible, just touch your knee with your hand.) Do this twelve times. Then do the homolateral (same side of the body) crawl. Swing your right arm and right leg forward in unison, then switch to your left arm and leg. You will need to hold onto a counter or table for balance. Do this twelve times on each side.

4. Then do the positive position; see instructions in Transformer 29.

5. Finally do the TATWA (Tapas Acupressure Technique With Affirmations), which can also be done on its own. See Transformer 15 for instructions.

When to Use This Transformer

The Bliss Method is great to use as a regular centring exercise. It is especially helpful if you are stuck on something and need to see things from a new perspective. It will help you get back on track. If it comes up when you open to that page in this chapter on Transformers, try it out and see how you feel afterward.

Does your energy need shifting?

Transformer 20—Magnet Exercise

When two magnets of opposing polarity meet, they are drawn together with a powerful force. Imagine what it is that you desire; feel all the feelings around this desire and see a huge magnet attached to this desire. Then feel the magnetic force in your heart area; a feeling of love and expansion that extends out from your heart. Visualize the two being drawn together by this magnetic force until they are united, just like two magnets when they come into contact with each other.

When to Use This Transformer

Use this technique when you want to manifest something into your life.

Time to bring it to you.

Transformer 21—Reach to the Heavens Stretch

Place one hand with palm facing the floor and the other with palm facing the heavens and push in each direction as hard as you can and look upwards. Then do the other side. If you can do this outside, it is more expansive. This is an easy stretch, but you will feel the pull in your back and chest and it helps open up the heart area.

When to Use This Transformer

If your heart is feeling constricted and you are experiencing some anger, it is helpful to focus on the heart and let go of any constriction that may be there. It is also good to do if you have spent a long time on the computer or in a confining space and need a good stretch. It's quick and easy, but very effective. It is also helpful with just taking time out and seeing things differently. Focus on the expansiveness of the sky and on seeing the bigger picture.

Time to see a new perspective and reach for the heavens.

Transformer 22—Calf Pump

This is a quick exercise that is a very effective stress release. When we are under stress our body activates the tendon guard reflex, tightening up the tendons behind the ankles, and our brain downshifts into reptilian mode. This exercise returns the tendons to normal tone and deactivates the stress response, which will release that deep fight or flight stress response.

To do this exercise, hold onto a counter or the back of a chair with both hands. Place one leg behind you and lean forward, bending the knee of the forward leg. Then press your heel to the floor, thereby stretching the calf, and shift your weight to your outstretched leg. Exhale while pressing the heel down. Repeat with the other side and do each leg three or more times.

When to Use This Transformer

Use this during times of stress or just to release any tension you are carrying.

You need to move forward as you are stuck in the past.

Transformer 23—Shoulder Points and Neck Points

Place both your hands on your shoulders (pinching the muscle) half way between the neck and shoulder. Rub your fingers into these spots. They may feel tender. This will help to loosen the tension in your shoulders and help them relax. Then place your thumb and index finger from one hand on the base of your skull in the soft spots and rub with a firm pressure. These exercises are more powerful when performed on you by another person, but they can also be effective when you do them yourself.

When to Use This Transformer

These points are great for headaches or for any tightness in your shoulders.

Are you carrying unnecessary burdens?
What are some new choices you can make to lessen them?

Transformer 24—Stepping Out of Chaos

I find this Transformer very powerful when I am caught up in all the "to dos" of life and my mind is running amok.

Take a deep breath and in your mind just take a step backward. Then another breath and another step backward. Keep doing this. With each step backward, just watch all the thoughts that come up and feel yourself stepping out of the chaos and into a place of only observing. This sounds really simple, but it can be quite powerful. Give it a try.

When to Use This Transformer

Use this any time you feel overwhelmed, or need to take an observer's role in your life and get out of the chaos.

Is your external world creating chaos in your life?

Transformer 25—Face Massage

This activity relaxes the face muscles and helps to relax the whole body. There are important acupressure points in the face and when pressure is applied to these areas, it can ignite a stress release response in your whole body. I find this one very helpful to do while relaxing in the bath. However, you can do this anywhere: at your desk, before you go to sleep, or anytime you need to relax.

Place the middle fingers of both hands on either side of the inside of the bridge of your nose and moved them up along the eyebrow line, applying a firm pressure and rubbing all the way around the outer eye along the cheekbone under your eye until you reach the tip of your nostrils. Place your middle fingers at the front centre of your hairline and gently rub along your hairline while moving your fingers down to the jaw, then to your chin. Then with one hand, do the "duck beak" by placing your thumb under your bottom lip and your index and middle fingers on your top lip. Rub both these points while pursing your lips (hence the name "duck beak").

Repeat as many times as needed (at least three times are helpful). Feel your body relaxing.

When to Use This Transformer

Use this whenever you feel any tension in your face or body.

What face are you presenting to the world?

Transformer 26—Balancing Buttons

Place one hand flat over the navel area. With the other hand, rub the kidney acupressure points, on either side of the sternum, just below the clavicles, by placing your thumb on one side and index finger on the other. Rub fairly vigorously. They may feel tender, but that will dissipate as you rub them. I have found this extremely effective in managing emotional issues. It helps to bring balance back to the system. It also helps to energize the brain as the carotid artery is behind these points and this stimulates oxygen to get to the brain.

When to Use This Transformer

This exercise is great before doing anything that requires more brain power, like writing an exam, or when you are caught up in an emotional issue and need to let go of tension around it.

Where is your life out of kilter?

Transformer 27—Create a Happy Thought for the Day

This one is so easy and is a great way to refocus the mind. At the beginning of the day, think of a wonderful thought that makes you happy, then tuck this thought in your pocket and, when your mind starts to go into a negative space, immediately shift gears and retrieve your happy thought.

This does take some practice but can really help you to dodge that negative train of thoughts.

When to Use This Transformer

This can be used anytime you want to shift from the negative to the positive.

Make a choice to be happy.

Transformer 28—Three Thumps

With your three middle fingers of one hand, vigorously tap the following points:

- K-27; these are the soft spots under the clavicles and on either side of the sternum);
- The thymus point (your upper chest area);
- The spleen points, which are four inches down from the armpit. Doing the chicken dance by tapping both fists on your sides will hit the right points.

When to Use This Transformer

This exercise will help re-energize the body, and can be very helpful if you are in an acute situation (like if you are having an allergic reaction to anything, you're really upset about something, or you're feeling exhausted). Keep tapping until the situation eases. I have seen this work so well when someone is having an allergic reaction to a food or to their environment.

You are doing too much and need to give your physical body a rest.

Transformer 29—PACE

This is an Educational Kinesiology technique that helps to integrate both lobes of the brain and balance brain chemistry.

1. PACE begins with water. Before you begin, drink some water.
2. Balancing Buttons (Kidney Buttons) This position is extremely effective in managing emotional issues. It helps to bring balance back to the system. It also helps to energize the brain, as the carotid artery is behind these points and this stimulates oxygen into the brain.
    A. Place one hand flat over the navel area. With the other hand rub the kidney acupressure points (K 27s) by placing your thumb on one side of your sternum and your index finger on the other, just below the clavicles. Rub fairly vigorously. They may feel tender, but this will dissipate as you rub.
3. Cross Crawl
    A. Do a cross crawl: In a standing position take your left elbow and touch your right knee, moving your whole body in that direction. Then go in the opposite direction. If this is not possible just touch your knee with your hand.
4. Positive Position (Brain Gym term Hook-ups) Cross your ankles and place your right arm over the left arm with palms facing down.
    A. Clasp your hands and then draw them underneath to your chest. (Like giving yourself a warm hug.) Sit for five minutes and just take deep breaths with your tongue pressed to the roof of your mouth (this connects to your central meridian). You can also use this time to say positive things to yourself such as, "I am relaxed and calm", or whatever works for you to make you feel better. End with hands together in a tent position and feet flat on the floor.

When to Use This Transformer

PACE can be great as a preventative tool to keep you balanced daily and it helps to integrate both lobes of the brain so you are more focused, clear-headed, and calm. It is amazing for any activity for which you need to be alert and have greater brain power, like an exam or an interview. It is also good for calming the brain and helping you to be more peaceful and centred. If you are on the computer a lot, then PACE helps to realign the brain after gazing at a flat surface. It is valuable too, for anyone with ADD or ADHD. When I was a social worker, I used this with kids, and it made amazing improvements in their focus and writing ability. When these skills were easier for them, it also improved their self-esteem.

Time for Inner balance.

Transformer 30—Changing Belief Patterns

State your limiting belief and then state its opposite: the belief you want to have. For example, the limiting belief "I am not good enough" becomes "I am good enough and can accomplish anything I desire".

Then do the cross crawl (see Transformer 29—PACE , above), as you say this new belief out loud for as long as it feels right . This will help realign the brain to this new positive thought.

When to Use This Transformer

Do this any time you want to change a limiting belief and reprogram the brain to a new belief. Sometimes, EFT may need to be done first and then locked in with this Transformer.

Is there an old belief that is keeping you
from expanding your present reality?

Transformers 31 to 40

Whereas the transformers above have some specific application, the following ones can be done whenever and as often as you feel so moved.

Transformer 31—Creating Personal Space

This may seem like an unusual Transformer and it isn't a tool per se, but it is worth noting that the space you occupy daily can really affect you in a positive (or negative) way. If you turn the pages of this book to this Transformer, then you may need to look at the space around you and ask yourself how it is making you feel. I think it is important to be surrounded by things that make you feel good. If your home is a mess, then what is your mind like? As I have mentioned, your thoughts mirror your external world and vice versa. So keep your external world calm with objects that evoke peace and make you feel good. Create a nourishing space for yourself. I quite often have candles lit during the day, and I buy flowers, which I love. Aromatherapy can also be a way of keeping you calm and changing your emotional state. A natural aromatherapy spray is part of my work attire. I don't leave home without it. The sense of smell has a powerful effect on the entire body.

Do your surroundings reflect how you want to feel?

Transformer 32—Music

There are numerous studies that have shown that music has a profound effect on the chemical composition of the brain. I personally use music all the time to get centred and just to feel good. It is amazing how easily it can change your mood and there is so much music to choose from. I have also seen how therapeutic music can be and what a powerful effect it has on me and others. When Denise Hagan—my friend who writes and sings her own music—sings, we always have Kleenex around. Her music opens up hearts and quite often evokes powerful emotions that can have a profound healing effect. Her website is www.denisehagan.com.

Music is a great way to centre yourself and open your heart. Find music that you resonate with. There is so much to choose from.

Express a different tune in your life.

Transformer 33—Celebrate

Take some time to celebrate what you have already accomplished. Send yourself a letter about how proud you are of yourself and list all that you have created. Plan a fun celebration with friends or whatever works for you. Let your imagination run wild. Have a party! Celebrate!

Time to enjoy your accomplishments and celebrate life.

Transformer 34—Calling in the Angels

This is a powerful Transformer and can lighten your load. Call in your angels and guides, whatever you are comfortable with. Tell them what you need. Be courageous and let go your load to higher guidance. Be willing to ask for what you need.

It's time to ask for Divine help.

Transformer 35—Get Your Creative Juices Going

Do some art, sing, or create a craft. Do something creative to get you out of the left-doing brain and into your right-creative brain. From this place you can be more open to inspiration and closer to your Divine essence. Remember not to judge yourself—everyone is creative, and it doesn't matter what your results look like—just show up, and let your creative energies flow.

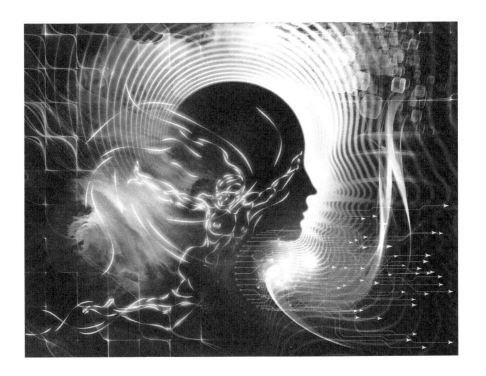

Create something beautiful from your heart.

Transformer 36—Opening the Doors to Your God Self

Get quiet and imagine you are in a room with four doors. Open each one and imagine the light from your God Self, the Source, flooding in. Go around your imaginary room and open each door. Feel yourself being filled with this amazing light and wisdom from all directions. I know this sounds rather simple, but I have had profound results and can feel the energy just surge through me when I do this.

When to Use This Transformer

This is good to use at night to fill your mind with positive energy before you go to dreamland, or anytime you want to connect to your God Self.

There is a greater power inside you than your mind can imagine.
Open up to this powerful force within.

Transformer 37—Giving

This has been the most powerful of all transformers in my own life. Giving of myself to others has taken me out of my own self-indulgence and into an open heart space that has uplifted my vibration. I get pure joy from giving. When we help others we are helping our selves. How can you help humanity in big or small ways? What contribution can you leave behind?

"I have found that among its other benefits, giving liberates the soul of the giver."
Maya Angelou

It is time to expand your awareness outside your own needs.

Transformer 38—Positive Points

This exercise will help you think more clearly. With one hand, place your thumb and middle finger on the bony protrusions on your forehead, in line with your eyeballs, half way between your eyebrows and your hairline. This draws the energy to be focused on the frontal lobe rather than on the reptilian brain, where energy is focused when we are stressed.

This exercise is more powerful when done by someone else, but can be effectively done by yourself.

When to Use This Transformer

Use this when you feel stressed and are in your reptilian brain (reacting with fight or flight). Try it sometime when your child is really upset. It can be a very effective way to calm them down. It's especially effective when something has just triggered you and you can feel your emotions reacting negatively or unconsciously.

Be kind to yourself and take time to just be.

Transformer 39—Group Activities

Joining a group of like-minded others in an activity that is soul-restoring can be such a gift to your mind, body, and spirit. Maybe it's Yoga, a knitting group, or a choir. It can be anything that you resonate with and will uplift your spirits. Have fun with this and let your mind take you totally outside the box. Pick something wild and fanciful or something you have been longing to do for a long time, but just haven't allowed yourself the time and space for it. Now is the time.

It is time to engage in a stress reliever.

Transformer 40—Seeking External Help

All the above Transformers are ones you can do alone or with a friend. They can be valuable tools in helping you move forward and helping you connect to your Divine nature. However, there are times when it may be necessary to seek external help. If you have opened to this page, then be honest with yourself and see if it feels right for you to get support from a professional, a family member, a spiritual counselor, an energy worker, or whomever. You may also just need to share with a close friend. Do what feels right; follow your inner guidance. If a therapy of some sort is what you need, then do your research. There are so many therapies and therapists out there. See which modality you resonate with and check out different therapists. Get a referral and ask someone who has seen this person what their experience has been. People can only take you to where they have gone themselves. You want someone who walks their talk!

Time to seek support from others.

In Closing

When we truly connect to our heart and our God essence, all else pales in comparison and in this place, we are an absolute channel for Divine intelligence. This is the place of miracles. This is what it truly means to get out of our own way. From this place we flow into the intelligence that has greater wisdom than our small ego minds and we can tap into immense information that can bring our dreams to realization. This is such a freeing and expansive place to reside in. From this place I feel like I can fly with the blue herons and can accomplish anything. My heart sings and expands and bliss fills every cell. This is what I am here on earth for. Then I become an absolute catalyst for good, because my Divine intelligence wants only good for others, just as I have created for myself. Then my dreams and desires are God choices, not ego's longings to make it feel better about itself; choices that are based on the collective, greater good that transforms my soul and helps to uplift all those around me.

Our journey is coming to a close. Thank you for sharing it with me. I hope you have found some of this information helpful. I would like to remind you that you are magnificent and a valuable part of creation. You deserve a wonderful life. So get out of your own way and let your Divine Self lead you to where you want to go! Remember, the more you are in awe, the more there is to be in awe about.

With kind thoughts,

Kristina

Afterword

How to Get Out of Your Own Way

I close my computer and I think the journey has ended. I have written the last word and I take a huge breath. Writing a book is an emotional journey and I have been totally immersed in the process. When it is complete, it feels as though there is a void and I'm not quite sure what to fill it with, that feeling of "Now what"? Little did I know it was only a beginning to something huge? A big shift in my consciousness.

For a couple of months after finishing writing, I felt let down and unsettled, and I didn't feel worthy of the words I had written. I was getting sick with colds and flus that normally I am not a host for. Many of the doors that I was trying to open during this time were closing, so this was a confirmation that I just needed to "be", to let it all unfold and stop the doing. I am grateful that I have learned that lesson and it doesn't take as long as it used to.

Even though this was a very challenging time, I could hear an inner voice deep inside, and I knew this was just a time of clearing old patterns and behaviours so I could really open up to what lay ahead. I sought support from external sources during this time; that was very helpful.

One of the treatments I used was B.E.S.T. (standing for Bio Energetic Synchronization Technique), which my chiropractor Dr. Christina Updegrove does so beautifully; you can find more information at www. morter.com. This work gets at the root of old patterns in the unconscious mind, patterns that affect the nervous system, and releases them. In addition to external support, I also listened to some great audios by metaphysical teachers on the internet, and of course did many of the transformers in this book, such as EFT so that I could be with all my feelings and gain the clarity I'd not had before.

Just sitting with things is not my comfort zone—as I have shared, my default mode is doing. I just needed to sit and reach deep inside for answers and have the courage to listen.

I had many epiphanies during this time, one of which was very profound. For a good part of my life I had no life line of knowing there is a creator inside of me that I can rely on. My limiting belief was "I have to do this on my own". Make the list and "get 'er done" was my motto. Though I had manifested some amazing things—it was harder than it needed to be. That life line of connecting to my God Self/the source of all creation, only came into my consciousness about twenty years ago, which really isn't that long. Old patterns and beliefs that create the personality were way older than that. Once I got that realization I could move to a place of acceptance of it all and become kinder and gentler with myself. That loosened the ego's grip and I could just witness the chaos I was feeling. I think a huge pain for many of us is that we think we are separate from creation/source, until we realize it is us. We are this powerful force within; we can relax and know we are supported.

This realization calmed the chaos and I was able to see that most of my life I had tried to "make" it happen. Now instead, I needed to listen to the voice of my God Self and "let" it happen. I had to "surrender", and surrender I did.

Break Down Quite Often Leads to Break Through

Another of my realizations was that I need to talk to my God Self more and really connect in an intimate way with this part of myself. Also a huge part of this process was journaling; or as my loving daughter-in-law affectionately calls it, "barf" journaling. This is when your hand can't move as fast as the speed with which all the insights come pouring out. So much excavating! Yikes! And here I thought I was done with all that digging. When you have a path to go on you have to dump the old stuff to open up space for the new; journaling can be that dumping ground.

One night after so much of this excavating and purging, I had the most profound dream I have ever had. It was strange, because as I was going to sleep I kept getting over and over "Something is going to happen tonight". I was almost expecting the phone to ring with some kind of message. Well, I finally fell asleep and had this dream.

It was a "rags to riches" kind of dream. I was wearing an old dress and a male figure arrived; he is currently a famous person in the United States.

There was such a deep connection and love between us. We were going to a conference together, and I was transformed like Cinderella from my ugly dress into a beautiful one. Then, during the dream this figure started to disappear. I knew he was dying and that I had to save him. He then transformed into a thin shield, which I placed in my solar plexus. I then saw three gold towers in the distance and knew that if I made it to those towers, we would be safe and he would live. I shot up through the air and could feel all obstacles bouncing off me. I felt so powerful and it felt so real. I knew this was coming from a place I had not experienced before. I made it to the golden towers and the male figure came alive again. When I awoke, I was saying "I have saved Asurat" and that my name was "Anoni". Later upon reflection, I realized that it was me that I was saving.

I knew something very powerful had just happened and life would be different. I felt a power I had not felt before. That feeling of shooting upward and having obstacles just bounce off me stayed with me and I can still feel the power of that dream.

Soon after that amazing experience, my friend and I were leaving for Africa and the transformation continued. Africa sure helped me open my eyes to what is really important. When I saw mothers getting up at 5:00 a.m. to walk five miles just to get water, it sure gave me a reality check. We were fortunate to stay right in a Maasai village, and dance, sing, and eat with the Maasai people. It was an amazing experience. Then we went to an orphanage where my friend and I fell in love with two little girls who opened up our hearts even wider. Doors are now wide open and so is my heart.

One thing I am the most grateful for is that I am no longer a seeker, but I know the truth of who I really am. I am source, divine intelligence, and part of the consciousness of all that is. My only task now is to support myself continually in getting out of my own way and surrender to being an expression of that truth.

Resource Section

Other Therapies

There are many therapies that can help you stay centered and focused, like Qigong, laughter Yoga, hatha yoga, etc., far too many to mention them all. If you resonate with one, then check it out. The following are a few websites for information:

www.acupressurevictoria.ca
www.purpletreehealingcentre.com
www.yogakat.ca
www.panachedesai.com
www.panachedesai.com/membership/

Brain Gym

The Brain Gym exercises in these Transformers come from Educational Kinesiology, which is based on an educational model emphasizing the interaction that takes place between all parts of the brain and the body. Educational Kinesiology uses movement to enhance the learning potential within each of us. Brain Gym works on learning challenges, but it is also very helpful for people with no overt learning difficulties. It works to bring about improvements in the ability to assimilate and recall information, often resulting in an increased capacity to learn. Goals for acquiring new abilities (for example, public speaking) are set, and appropriate exercises are done to help the brain develop and use new pathways for learning.

Website: www.braingym.org

Mr. Gregg Braden

Contact information for anyone who may have questions about Gregg Braden's work is as follows:

Wisdom Traditions

Office of Gregg Braden
PO Box 14668
North Palm Beach, Florida 33408
561.799.9337
Fx: 561.799.9343
info@greggbraden.com
www.greggbraden.com

Health Kinesiology
www.hk-training.org/Dr.Jimmy-Scott-Ph.D.html

Author Biography

Kristina Sisu trained as a Social Worker and became a Certified Nutritionist, a Specialized Kinesiologist, and an Energy Worker. Her personal experience and triumph over a serious, chronic illness prompted her to share her passion for issues of health and well-being with others.

In 2006, she left her private practice and corporate wellness work and followed a dream to be a flight attendant; she moved to Canada's West Coast. Kristina is now living in Victoria, British Columbia, Canada and following her passion of supporting others in living their dreams and realizing their own magnificence.

She is the author of *Food and the Emotional Connection*.

About the Author

Kristina has been in the wellness field as a Teacher, Key Note Presenter, Workshop Facilitator and Private Practitioner for over 20 years. Her style of presenting has been described as:

"Compassionate" "Enthusiastic" "Energetic" "Inspiring" "Engaging"

Her story of healing her illness has brought hope to many others and her skills as a therapist have supported many in releasing blocks and moving forward with their lives.

"The treatment you gave me was very transformational. I have to say..I really felt like I was myself for the first time ever. I feel like it is something I need to connect with regularly so I can feel healthy emotionally."
Sherri, Ontario

"All week I could feel a difference. Depression and negative thoughts have lifted and I feel lighter again. Quite amazing actually."
Kathy, Victoria, BC

Kristina is the owner of Higher Ground

Services provided:
* Change Sessions
* Intuitive Readings (both available via internet)
* Ion Foot Cleanses
* Rife Technology

She is also the Author of *"Food and the Emotional Connection"*

Visit www.KristinaSisu.com for more information and join her mailing list to receive her Higher Ground Newsletter.

KristinaSisu@gmail.com

If you want to get on the path to be a published author by
Influence Publishing please go to
www.InfluencePublishing.com/inspireabook/

Inspiring books that influence change

More information on our other titles and how to submit
your own proposal can be found at
www.InfluencePublishing.com

CPSIA information can be obtained at www.ICGtesting.com
Printed in the USA
LVOW01s2026200514

386628LV00001B/1/P